An Overview of THE NEW TESTAMENT

An Overview of THE NEW TESTAMENT

JOHN MALSEED

AMG Publishers

Following God Through the Bible: An Overview of the New Testament
Revised Edition

Copyright © 2003 by John Malseed
Revised Edition © 2008 by John Malseed

Published by AMG Publishers
6815 Shallowford Rd.
Chattanooga, Tennessee 37421

All rights reserved. Except for brief quotations in printed reviews, no part of this publication may be reproduced, stored in a retrieval system or transmitted in any form or by any means (printed, written, photocopied, visual electronic, audio, or otherwise) without the prior permission of the publisher.

Unless otherwise indicated, all Scripture quotations are taken from the HOLY BIBLE, NEW INTERNATIONAL VERSION®. NIV®. Copyright ©1973, 1978, 1984 by International Bible Society. Used by permission of Zondervan Publishing House. All rights reserved.

ISBN 0-89957-266-9

Revised edition (Second printing)—March 2008

Cover designed by ImageWright, Inc., Chattanooga, Tennessee

Edited and Proofread by Christine Andrepont, Dan Penwell, Rick Steele, and Robert Malseed

Printed in Canada

14 13 12 11 10 09 08 -T- 9 8 7 6 5 4 3 2

DEDICATION

To my wife, Helen,

Who lifted me from the theological plain to the practical.

Contents

Acknowledgments

I am deeply grateful to Paul Bootes of Koorong Books for introducing me to AMG Publishers, to Graeme Murray for encouraging me to commence the project, to John Brain for helping with the original layout, to Andrew Tilsley for reigniting the flame, to Dan Penwell of AMG Publishers for continued encouragement, accessibility, and brilliant ideas, to Helen Colquhoun for friendship, encouragement, and prayer support, to Sid Bacon who encouraged me in the pursuit of excellence, and to my family for their continued support.

Kudos also go to Adrian Bain for his format design and to Eric Hook who made templates enabling me to use this new format. I am also thankful to Rick Steele of AMG Publishers for his advice and his support for this revised edition.

A special acknowledgement is due to Robert Malseed of Albuquerque, New Mexico. Though only a distant relation in the flesh, he is a brother in the Lord. I discovered him via his web site (www.malseed.com) several years ago. Since then we have visited each other as well as our common ancestral home in Ireland. Robert used the published first edition of this book in daily devotion time and provided me with numerous suggestions for a revised edition. He then did the same for *An Overview of The Old Testament* before it was published. I was so pleased with that book I determined to revise this New Testament study. We set up a system whereby I would enter the text into the new format, email it to Robert for review, and we would then spend hours discussing and editing the book. He contributed a few additional questions for the studies. The final collaboration process was enabled thanks to Robert helping to set up our computers and instant messaging audio connection so that we could simultaneously talk and work in Australia and in New Mexico, USA.

To my knowledge I have not unwittingly taken directly from any source. As ideas came to mind, I formed the questions. Yet, to all those Christian writers and speakers from whom I have gleaned knowledge and understanding over the years, and who it is now impossible to remember, I acknowledge with humble thanks.

Introduction

Every Christian conference I attended, from the time I was first converted to Christ, emphasized the importance of daily Bible study. I realized that to grow in the knowledge of God and to fulfill God's purpose for one's life a disciplined approach to understanding His Word was required. I can remember buying a notebook, sharpening a pencil, and taking the Bible down from the shelf to begin a Bible study. I can't remember writing anything down; I had nothing to guide me.

Following God Through the Bible: An Overview of the New Testament is a chapter-by-chapter guide of the Bible, which helps the student study the Bible rather than studying books about the Bible. Its main purpose is to allow the reader to discover biblical truths by himself or herself with the Holy Spirit's help. Scripture is its own interpreter so that by comparing Scripture with Scripture you can discover the message God has just for you. ***Following God Through the Bible*** does not give answers to the questions asked, the answers are in the textbook—the Bible.

Each section and series of questions have the following purposes:

- As a guide to make the study of Scripture easier and thus, motivate you.
- To help make the Scripture relevant to your daily life.
- To challenge you to learn the great doctrines of the Bible by searching out other Scriptures.

This study guide has many different uses:

1. **Individuals can use it as daily study guide.**
   - The Outline Section gives a bird's-eye view of the chapter(s) content.
   - The Self-Examination Questions assist in this bird's-eye view by putting the context of the Bible into a more practical form.
   - The Context Questions will help you understand the section in greater detail by honing-in on points that are often missed.
   - The Research Study Questions challenge the individual to search the Scriptures for answers, comparing one Scripture with another Scripture.
   - The Prayer and Praise Section allows for a time of quiet heart searching in which to praise God, ask for help, and contemplate the lessons of the study.

2. Classes and study groups can use it as a group study guide.

Each group member can work on the chapter questions at home. And when they assemble as a group, they can discuss their answers. In the group setting, the leader can divide the chapter into sections and draw from the section's reflective questions as a basis for discussion.

3. Pastors can use the study guide as a basis for homiletic sermons and lessons. Because each chapter of the New Testament has been divided into sections with the contents outlined, there is ample material for allowing these studies to become the basis for a sermon or a series of sermons.

The aim of ***Following God Through the Bible: An Overview of the New Testament*** is to open up the Word of God. The *questions* asked are just the tool for understanding; the *answers* are where the rubber meets the road.

Matthew 1

Jesus, son of David, son of Abraham, is virgin born.

Read prayerfully the following sections.

Ch. 1:1–6	Matthew reviews the generations from Abraham to David.
Ch. 1:7–11	Matthew reviews the generations from David to the exile.
Ch. 1:12–17	Matthew reviews the generations from the exile to the birth of Christ.
Ch. 1:18–25	Matthew reviews the angel's instructions regarding Jesus' birth.

Review the passage and answer these context questions.

Who was David's great grandmother?

What are the names given to Mary's child in this chapter?

What part did Joseph have in the birth of Jesus?

Research study questions; refer to scripture cross-references.

What was unusual about the five women included in the genealogy? Gen. 38; Josh. 2; Ruth 2; 2 Sam. 11; Matt. 1.

Why might "Jeconiah" be counted twice, taking into consideration the periods of his reign? 1 Chron. 3:16, 17; Jer. 22:30.

How important was it that Jesus should be virgin born? Is. 7:14; Rom. 5:12–17.

Record your answer to these self-examination questions.

How do I treat those who come from a different ethnic background?

What is my attitude toward those who have wronged me?

When did I first realize God's purpose in sending Jesus?

Respond to God in prayer and praise.

Ask to understand how God can use the unlikely. Ask for a willingness to obey God. Praise God for sending Jesus to save us from our sins.

Matthew 2

Jesus is worshipped by the Magi, but Herod seeks His destruction.

Read prayerfully the following sections.

Ch. 2:1–12	Wise men worship Jesus and are interviewed by wrathful Herod.
Ch. 2:13–15	Angel warns Joseph and Mary to escape to Egypt.
Ch. 2:16–18	Herod's wrath signs the death warrant for all male children.
Ch. 2:19–23	Herod wastes away and dies; Jesus' family returns to Nazareth.

Review the passage and answer these context questions.

What sort of person were the wise men hoping to find?

How long was Joseph commanded to stay in Egypt?

How many times did Joseph demonstrate his obedience?

Research study questions; refer to scripture cross-references.

What indicates that the wise men came to visit Jesus much later than His birth in the manger? Matt. 2:11.

There is much mystery regarding who these wise men were and where they came from. How do the following verses center our attention on who they came to see and what they came to do? Ps. 72:9–11; Is. 60:1–3.

Herod's plan was to kill Jesus, but the scriptures already foretold that Jesus would be moved to Nazareth. How were these scriptures fulfilled? Hos. 11:1; Mic. 5:2.

Record your answer to these self-examination questions.

What gifts do I bring to Jesus as I bow before Him in worship?

How obedient am I to God's call when He asks me to change locations?

When tragedies strike, do I blame God or seek understanding of His will?

Respond to God in prayer and praise.

Ask for greater alertness to respond to the intervention of God.
Ask for protection from the anger of ungodly people. Ask for wisdom to identify the voice of God.

Matthew 3

John the Baptist comes preaching and then baptizes Jesus.

Read prayerfully the following sections.

Ch. 3:1–6	John comes preaching repentance, and many respond and are baptized.
Ch. 3:7–12	The religious come and are warned of judgment.
Ch. 3:13–17	Jesus comes to be baptized by John in the Jordan.

Review the passage and answer these context questions.

What was the effect of John's preaching?

In the context, what did the baptism of fire entail?

Why did Jesus submit to the rite of baptism?

Research study questions; refer to scripture cross-references.

What would indicate that John's message of repentance meant a radical change in life? 2 Cor. 5:17.

Why might John's condemnation of the Pharisees and Sadducees arise from the fact that he knew they were only performing their religious duties as a ritual? Who else recognized them as deceitful and hypocritical? Matt. 23:27.

What resolution was Jesus fulfilling by submitting to baptism? Ps. 40:6–8.

Record your answer to these self-examination questions.

What is my response to the message of repentance? Have I confessed my sin?

How conscious am I that man-made religion brings no hope of salvation?

How can I be truly humble as I do God's work?

Respond to God in prayer and praise.

Ask for greater courage to preach repentance.
Ask for the filling of the Holy Spirit. Praise God for the Father's gift of His Son.

Matthew 4

Jesus is tempted and then begins preaching and calling disciples.

Read prayerfully the following sections.

Ch. 4:1–11	Jesus fasts for forty days and gains victory over Satan.
Ch. 4:12–17	Jesus fulfills prophecy by returning to Galilee.
Ch. 4:18–22	Jesus finds four men fishing and calls them.
Ch. 4:23–25	Jesus focuses on the sick and continues teaching.

Review the passage and answer these context questions.

Who were the spiritual entities present at Jesus' temptations?

What motivated Jesus to move to Capernaum?

What promise did Jesus make to the brothers, Andrew and Peter?

Research study questions; refer to scripture cross-references.

How do these verses suggest that Satan was asking Jesus to act independently of the Word of God? Ps. 40:7, 8; John 4:34.

What other examples show that Satan was attempting to destroy the humanity of Christ? Matt. 1:18–20; 2:16–18; John 8:59.

What scripture states that Satan is the prince of this world? When will the kingdoms of this world be given to Jesus? John 12:31; 2 Cor. 4:4; Rev. 11:15.

Record your answer to these self-examination questions.

In what way can I use the Scriptures to overcome temptation?

What do I learn about preaching from Jesus?

When Jesus calls, what should my response be?

Respond to God in prayer and praise.

Praise God for the light of the gospel. Ask for a responsive heart when Jesus calls. Ask for greater opportunities to bring others to Jesus.

Matthew 5

Jesus teaches disciples concerning righteousness in His kingdom.

Read prayerfully the following sections.

Ch. 5:1–16	Jesus explains the characteristics and blessings of the kingdom.
Ch. 5:17–20	Jesus exposes the false righteousness of the Pharisees.
Ch. 5:21–48	Jesus expands what the Law says on six important subjects.

Review the passage and answer these context questions.

What should the believer do when persecuted?

When the gospel is shared, what will men do?

What does swearing entail according to the context?

Research study questions; refer to scripture cross-references.

List some things salt is used for. How can these be applied to Christian living? Col. 4:6.

When Jesus speaks of adultery, He is referring to both the seventh and tenth commandments. What was He saying? Ex. 20:14, 17; Col. 3:5; 1 Thess. 4:3.

In the "eye for eye" and "tooth for tooth" teaching, is Jesus adding further restriction to what the Law allowed? Ex. 21:22–26.

Record your answer to these self-examination questions.

What is my attitude toward the Bible, others, the world, and myself?

Who teaches me, and what enables me to fulfill the Law in my daily living?

How am I putting into practice what Jesus said concerning hate, lust, revenge, etc.?

Respond to God in prayer and praise.

Ask to have the qualities of kingdom citizens. Ask for Christ's righteousness to be seen in you. Ask for personal integrity in word, thought, and action.

Matthew 6—7

Jesus continues the discourse on true righteousness, using practical themes.

Read prayerfully the following sections.

Ch. 6:1–18	Jesus teaches that personal devotions should be exercised in private.
Ch. 6:19–34	Jesus testifies that worrying about personal wealth is futile.
Ch. 7:1–23	Jesus tersely warns about judging others before looking at ourselves.
Ch. 7:24–29	Jesus tells a parable on the foundations of Christian living.

Review the passage and answer these context questions.

What are the dangers of accumulating wealth?

Why are we instructed not to worry?

What does Jesus call a person who is quick to judge?

Research study questions; refer to scripture cross-references.

Is there a danger that fasting, without prayer and Bible study, could be detrimental rather than beneficial in the Christian experience? Col. 2:23.

Is it right to take the words "do not worry about tomorrow" to mean not to make plans or provision for the future? 1 Tim. 5:8.

What can be learned about discernment in sharing the gospel from the references to "dogs" and "pigs"? Matt. 10:14; 21:23–27; Luke 23:9; Acts 13:44–51.

Record your answer to these self-examination questions.

What is my motive when I give away money?

How does worry help? Where do I find the fortitude not to worry?

In what way am I judging other people? Do I turn a blind eye to my own failings?

Respond to God in prayer and praise.

Ask for more help both to pray and forgive.
Ask for a greater commitment to Jesus. Praise God for answered prayer.

Matthew 8

Jesus demonstrates His power through performing many miracles.

Read prayerfully the following sections.

Ch. 8:1–13	Jesus cleanses a leper and heals a centurion's servant.
Ch. 8:14–22	Jesus cures Peter's mother-in-law and speaks of the cost of following.
Ch. 8:23–27	Jesus calms the stormy sea.
Ch. 8:28–34	Jesus casts out evil spirits from two demon-possessed men.

Review the passage and answer these context questions.

What lesson can be learned from the leper who came to Jesus?

What lesson can be learned from the centurion who came to Jesus?

What lesson can be learned about half-hearted discipleship?

Research study questions; refer to scripture cross-references.

Why did Jesus request that the healed leper tell no one about the miracle? Matt. 16:1; Luke 4:23; John 4:48.

What expression does Malachi use instead of "from the east to the west"? Mal. 1:11.

What do these verses say about self-denial, service, and suffering? Luke 9:23; Acts 16:31–34.

Record your answer to these self-examination questions.

In what way am I reaching out to the less fortunate to bring them healing?

How willing am I to make sacrifices to follow Christ?

When has the work of Christ cost me financially?

Respond to God in prayer and praise.

Praise God for the cleansing Jesus brings. Ask for a heart to follow without hesitation. Ask for liberation from besetting sins.

Matthew 9

Jesus continues His work by performing more miracles of healing.

Read prayerfully the following sections.

Ch. 9:1–13	Jesus has compassion on a paralytic and calls Matthew.
Ch. 9:14–22	Jesus is challenged on fasting and encourages a woman's faith.
Ch. 9:23–38	Jesus calls death to life, then catches the cry of the blind.

Review the passage and answer these context questions.

What motivated Jesus to heal the paralytic?

What kind of people did Jesus call to follow Him?

What is the Lord's solution to the lack of laborers in the harvest field?

Research study questions; refer to scripture cross-references.

What does it say about putting one's problems in the Lord's hands? 1 Peter 5:7.

Who does the "Lord of the Harvest" refer to? John 16:8–11.

Why is it harder to say "your sins are forgiven you" than to heal a person physically? Matt. 8:16; 12:15; Acts 16:31.

Record your answer to these self-examination questions.

Do I show compassion for others, or is monetary gain my primary interest?

When asked to keep confidences, how trustworthy am I?

What damage can I cause by gossiping?

Respond to God in prayer and praise.

Ask for the assurance that you have God's forgiveness.
Praise God that He calls sinners. Ask for eyes and ears touched by Jesus.

Matthew 10

Jesus sends out His twelve disciples to preach with His authority.

Read prayerfully the following sections.

Ch. 10:1–15	Jesus instructs the Twelve regarding their purpose, provision, and parish.
Ch. 10:16–23	Jesus instructs the disciples regarding persecution after His departure.
Ch. 10:24–42	Jesus instructs the disciples regarding courage and relationships.

Review the passage and answer these context questions.

What commission was given to the Twelve?

What command applies to us today?

What did Jesus mean when He said, "Whoever loses his life for my sake will find it"?

Research study questions; refer to scripture cross-references.

Why did Jesus give such strict instructions on what the disciples were to take with them on their missionary endeavours? Matt. 6:19–24; 1 Cor. 9:7–14.

Does the statement, "He who stands firm to the end will be saved," mean believers can lose their salvation? Rom. 8:38, 39; Eph. 2:8, 9; 1 Peter 1:4, 5.

Who is the one to be feared mentioned in verse 28? Is. 8:12, 13; Heb.10:31.

Record your answer to these self-examination questions.

In what way am I trusting God for provisions if called on to serve Him in full-time Christian ministry?

How can I show dependence on the Holy Spirit, who has been freely given?

How willing am I to break relationships for the sake of sharing the gospel?

Respond to God in prayer and praise.

Ask for the ability not to worry about how to speak for Jesus.
Praise God for the value He puts on us. Ask for a willingness to serve God.

Matthew

Jesus declares Himself to be the Messiah and denounces the unrepentant.

Read prayerfully the following sections.

Ch. 11:1–19	Jesus deals with John the Baptist's doubts.
Ch. 11:20–24	Jesus denounces unrepentant cities.
Ch. 11:25–30	Jesus discourses with the Father and calls the weary to rest.

Review the passage and answer these context questions.

What was John the Baptist's ministry?

What is the result of rejecting the message of repentance?

What is the result of coming to Jesus?

Research study questions; refer to scripture cross-references.

Why would Jesus say that John the Baptist would be least in the kingdom?

Why were Sodom and Gomorrah used to shame these cities?

In the church's experience how can learned men come to Christ? 1 Cor. 1:26–31.

Record your answer to these self-examination questions.

What is the best way to deal with doubts?

What miracle do I expect to convince me to repent?

In what way do I show my willingness to repent and turn back to God?

Respond to God in prayer and praise.

Pray for help to overcome doubts and fears. Praise God that He has led you to repentance. Ask for an understanding of the rest that Jesus offers.

Matthew 12

Jesus is presented as the Messiah but the Pharisees reject Him.

Read prayerfully the following sections.

Ch. 12:1–21	Jesus declares Himself to be Lord of the Sabbath.
Ch. 12:22–37	Jesus delivers a possessed man and is denounced by the Pharisees.
Ch. 12:38–50	Jesus details to the religious that He is greater than Jonah or Solomon.

Review the passage and answer these context questions.

Why could Jesus not break the law of the Sabbath?

Jesus was coming as a king according to Isaiah, but what kind of king would He be?

Whom did Jesus say He was greater than?

Research study questions; refer to scripture cross-references.

Is the unpardonable sin the rejection of the Holy Spirit's ministry in convicting men and pointing them to the Savior? Are there other possibilities? John 16:5–11.

What is the significance of "the sign of Jonah"? Matt. 12:40.

What added information does Luke give on Jesus' mother and brothers? Luke 8:21.

Record your answer to these self-examination questions.

Am I more interested in rituals than a relationship with God?

What good things are being drawn out of my life as a result of my deliverance?

In what way could I leave myself vulnerable to being oppressed by evil spirits?

Respond to God in prayer and praise.

Praise God that He breaks the power of Satan.
Ask for help to do the will of God.

Matthew 13:1-52

Jesus reveals the mysteries of the kingdom in parables.

Read prayerfully the following sections.

Ch. 13:1–23	Jesus relates the Parable of the Sower and explains the outcome.
Ch. 13:24–43	Jesus recites several parables, revealing the plan of Satan.
Ch. 13:44–52	Jesus will redeem, restore, and reclaim His kingdom.

Review the passage and answer these context questions.

Who do the wayside hearers represent?

Who do the rocky place hearers represent?

Who do the thorny ground hearers represent?

What does the good soil illustrate?

Research study questions; refer to scripture cross-references.

Satan is a master at counterfeiting. List some of his recorded strategies. Gal. 1:6–9; 2 Thess. 2:1–12; Rev. 2:9.

Leaven or yeast is used to illustrate the corruption of sin in the New Testament. What do the following references and pictures illustrate? Matt. 16:6–12; Luke 12:1; 1 Cor. 5:6–8.

Who was the prophet Jesus was referring to in verse 35? Ps. 78.

Record your answer to these self-examination questions.

How can I prepare my thinking to receive the Word of God and produce fruit?

How can I prevent Satan's false teaching from permeating my life?

What plans can I make to provide for others?

Respond to God in prayer and praise.

Thank God for the ability to hear the Word of God. Praise God for physical eyes that see and ears that hear. Ask for greater wisdom to know where your real treasure is.

Matthew 13:53—14:36

Jesus withdraws from His hometown and then performs two miracles.

Read prayerfully the following sections.

Ch. 13:53—14:12	John's witness is eliminated by wicked King Herod.
Ch. 14:13–21	Jesus withdraws but then willingly feeds a multitude.
Ch. 14:22–36	Jesus walks on water, and the disciples worship Him.

Review the passage and answer these context questions.

What indicates that Herod remained distressed over the killing of John?

How many people did Jesus feed at this time?

Why were the disciples afraid when they saw Jesus walking on the water?

Research study questions; refer to scripture cross-references.

Was this Herod Antipas' last opportunity to believe in Christ? How did he respond the second time? Luke 23:5–12.

What evidence did the disciples have, while in their boat, that should have assured them of the compassion of Jesus? Matt. 14:20–22.

Peter had "a little faith" while on the rough waters. What equipment is required in times of difficulty? Eph. 6:10–18.

Record your answer to these self-examination questions.

How can my sin and unlawful acts lead to the destruction of others?

How can the little I have to give bring blessing and satisfaction to others?

When has doubt and lack of faith caused me to sink in life's storms?

Respond to God in prayer and praise.

Pray for the wisdom not to take an oath when the outcome is unsure. Ask for bread to distribute to the hungry. Praise God for daily bread.

Matthew 15

Jesus condemns hypocrisy, heals Canaanite, and shows compassion on a crowd.

Read prayerfully the following sections.

Ch. 15:1–20	Jesus refutes the Pharisees' claim against His disciples.
Ch. 15:21–28	Jesus hears the cry of the Canaanite woman and cures her child.
Ch. 15:29–39	Jesus captivates the crowd and then feeds four thousand.

Review the passage and answer these context questions.

What were the Pharisees guilty of in the eyes of Jesus?

What sin did Jesus see in the disciples?

How did Jesus show His compassion for the crowd at this time?

Research study questions; refer to scripture cross-references.

Part of the Pharisees' tradition was to will their wealth to the temple and thus, excusing themselves from family responsibilities. Which commandment did Jesus say they were corrupting? Deut. 5:16; 27:16.

Why did the disciples request that Jesus send the Canaanite woman away? Did they have scriptural reason to do so? Matt. 10:1–6; John 3:16.

How did the disciples fail when they wanted to send the multitude away hungry? Matt. 14:31; John 2:5.

Record your answer to these self-examination questions.

What legalistic traditions prevent me from true worship and turns others away?

How persistent am I in asking the Lord's help? What can I say?

In what way can I provide for the physical needs of people?

Respond to God in prayer and praise.

Ask for a greater love for others. Praise God for His gospel to all nations. Praise God for Jesus, the Bread of Life.

Matthew 16

Jesus rebukes the religious, blesses Peter, and predicts His own death.

Read prayerfully the following sections.

Ch. 16:1–4	Jesus rebukes the religious crowd as they try to entrap Him.
Ch. 16:5–12	Jesus reminds the disciples about false teachers.
Ch. 16:13–20	Jesus reveals His identity and commends Simon Peter.
Ch. 16:21–28	Jesus reprimands Peter and predicts His own death.

Review the passage and answer these context questions.

What did the disciples lack when worrying about bread?

Who revealed to Peter that Jesus was the Messiah?

What indications in Peter's behavior showed that he was no different from the others?

Research study questions; refer to scripture cross-references.

How many times did the Pharisees and Sadducees ask Jesus for a sign? Matt. 12:38; 16:1; John 2:18; 6:30.

Is it important to understand that Jesus uses two different Greek words for rock—the first one translated "Peter," meaning "a stone" the second translated "rock," meaning that Jesus, Himself, is the foundation rock? Why? Eph. 2:19–22; 1 Pet. 2:4–8.

What terms does Peter use to describe himself? 1 Peter 1:1; 5:1; 2 Peter 1:1.

Record your answer to these self-examination questions.

What is the only sure way of judging the teaching I am exposed to?

How have I acknowledged Jesus as the Son of God?

In what ways can I deny myself to follow Jesus?

Respond to God in prayer and praise.

Ask for guidance to stay clear of legalism. Praise God that He is building His Church. Pray for grace as you deny yourself and follow Christ.

Matthew 17

Jesus is transfigured, treats demon possessed, and subscribes to temple tax.

Read prayerfully the following sections.

Ch. 17:1–13	Jesus is transfigured and talks to Moses and Elijah.
Ch. 17:14–23	Jesus transforms a demon possessed boy and teaches His disciples faith.
Ch. 17:24–27	Jesus tells Peter to pay two drachma temple tax.

Review the passage and answer these context questions.

What was heaven's message to the three disciples?

Why could the disciples not heal the demon possessed?

Why did Jesus pay the temple tax?

Research study questions; refer to scripture cross-references.

When will all believers see Jesus in His glory? 1 John 1:1–3; Rev. 19.

What kind of power is available through great faith? Matt. 17:20; John 14:12.

Jews in the royal family did not have to pay tax. In one sense, Jesus was in the royal family. Did Jesus ask Peter to pay taxes so as not to offend anyone? Matt. 22:15–22.

Record your answer to these self-examination questions.

When have I glorified other people to the detriment of Jesus?

In what way can my "little faith" grow into greater faith?

How often do I appropriate God's promises to supply my needs?

Respond to God in prayer and praise.

Pray for eyes to see the glories of Christ. Pray for more trust in God when things seem impossible. Thank God for His many blessings.

Matthew 18

Jesus teaches that true humility comes at great cost.

Read prayerfully the following sections.

Ch. 18:1–14	Jesus teaches that we should be humble and become as children.
Ch. 18:15–20	Jesus teaches that true humility requires difficult decisions.
Ch. 18:21–35	Jesus teaches that true humility requires us to forgive.

Review the passage and answer these context questions.

What was Jesus' actual reply to the disciples' question?

Did the shepherd care about those sheep that were not lost?

How many times was Peter prepared to forgive?

Research study questions; refer to scripture cross-references.

What ideas in these verses suggest that the world's greatest sin is causing people to reject Christ? 2 Cor. 4:3, 4; 2 Thess. 2:10.

Is Jesus teaching by shock? Would it not be better to lose a limb or an eye than to miss out on salvation? Luke 9:25; Rev. 20:7–15.

Why should believers seek to settle their differences? 1 Cor. 6:1–9.

Record your answer to these self-examination questions.

How often have I belittled those whose faith is new? How does mine compare?

How should I respond in a situation where I feel a brother is at fault?

How does God expect me to forgive and what is my position if I don't?

Respond to God in prayer and praise.

Ask for grace to bow humbly before God.
Praise God that He, with our help, is seeking the lost sheep.
Pray for grace to forgive others who may not deserve it.

Matthew 19

Jesus gives guidance on marriage, welcomes children and instructs a rich young ruler.

Read prayerfully the following sections.

Ch. 19:1–12	Jesus discourses with Pharisees on divorce and adultery.
Ch. 19:13–15	Jesus disapproves of disciples in disregarding little children.
Ch. 19:16–30	Jesus discusses with the rich ruler the cost of discipleship.

Review the passage and answer these context questions.

What was the extent of the Pharisees' question?

How did Jesus show His love for little children?

What was flawed about the rich man's question?

Research study questions; refer to scripture cross-references.

The Pharisees were trying to trap Jesus on the subject of divorce. Were they trying to get Jesus to take a liberal view on divorce so that they could condemn Him for distorting the Law? Or, had Christ offered the strict view, would they have accused Him of rejecting Deuteromy 24? Mark 10:2–9; 1 Cor. 7:1–15.

Was this rich man rejecting Jesus? Did Jesus trap this Jewish man by using the weapon usually used against Him, that is, the Law?

Record your answer to these self-examination questions.

Am I willing to heed Jesus' teaching, or am I following the trends of today?

If I have disobeyed, will I seek forgiveness and rededicate my situation to Him?

What efforts am I making to lead children to Jesus?

Respond to God in prayer and praise.

Pray for help to understand the commitment of marriage.
Praise God that He welcomes little children. Ask for help to observe God's commandments.

Matthew 20

Jesus relates the payment parable, predicts His death, and shows pity to two blind men.

Read prayerfully the following sections.

Ch. 20:1–16	Jesus preaches on the parable of the vineyard.
Ch. 20:17–19	Jesus predicts His betrayal, death, and resurrection.
Ch. 20:20–28	Jesus points to servanthood as He corrects a mother's ambition.
Ch. 20:29–34	Jesus shows compassion on two blind men by restoring their sight.

Review the passage and answer these context questions.

In the parable of the vineyard, was the landlord fair?

What lessons are learned from the mother's foolish request?

How did the blind men address Jesus?

Research study questions; refer to scripture cross-references.

When will Christians receive their rewards? Rom. 14:10; 1 Cor. 3:11–16; 2 Cor. 5:10.

What sort of crowns could Christians receive? 1 Thess. 2:19; 2 Tim. 4:7, 8; Jam. 1:12; 1 Pet. 5:4.

What was the mother of James and John ignorant of? What does the following scripture say about Christ's servanthood? Phil. 2.

Record your answer to these self-examination questions.

How often have I been resentful of others' rewards?

How prepared am I for the will of God to be fulfilled whatever the cost?

In what way do I practice being a servant to others?

Respond to God in prayer and praise.

Ask for contentment in knowing that God is sovereign.
Praise God for His plan of salvation. Ask for help to take the servant's place.

Matthew 21

Jesus triumphantly enters Jerusalem, transforms the temple, and teaches parables.

Read prayerfully the following sections.

Ch. 21:1–11	Jesus comes to Jerusalem, and crowds cover the road with their cloaks.
Ch. 21:12–17	Jesus cleanses the temple and casts out moneychangers.
Ch. 21:18–27	Jesus curses the fig tree and calls disciples to pray.
Ch. 21:28–46	Jesus cites two parables directed at the chief priests and Pharisees.

Review the passage and answer these context questions.

What happens that shows Jesus is the Prince of Peace?

What might indicate that the owner of the donkey was one of Jesus' followers?

What promise of faith did Jesus give?

Research study questions; refer to scripture cross-references.

What from the following verses might suggest that the crowd was only acknowledging Jesus because they wanted Him to get rid of the Romans? Zech. 9:9–17.

If the fig tree represents Israel as a nation, what fruit did Jesus find? Is. 5:1–7.

What is the lesson in the parable of the two sons? Which one gave lip service, and which one repented? Which one was honored?

Record your answer to these self-examination questions.

When have I showed willingness to obey God in service?

What fruit am I producing? Is there a danger my tree is withering?

In what ways do I serve God?

Respond to God in prayer and praise.

Hosanna to the Son of David! Hosanna in the highest! Pray for a greater willingness to work in God's vineyard. Praise God for His marvelous work in salvation.

Matthew 22

Jesus tells a parable about a wedding while Pharisees/Sadducees test Him.

Read prayerfully the following sections.

Ch. 22:1–14	In this parable, a King's invited guests refuse invitation so outsiders are invited.
Ch. 22:15–22	Jesus is informed of intent to trap Him over internal revenue.
Ch. 22:23–40	Jesus indicts the Sadducees as they err over doctrine.
Ch. 22:41–46	Jesus indicates to the Pharisees that He is the infinite God.

Review the passage and answer these context questions.

What had the man without the wedding garment forgotten to do?

In what way were the Pharisees trying to trap Jesus?

What are the two greatest commandments?

Research study questions; refer to scripture cross-references.

Name some servants that God has already sent to invite guests to His wedding banquet. What garment do I need to be one of His guests? Is. 64:6; Rom. 2:12, 13; 4:3; 5:19; 10:3.

Could Jesus' words regarding Caesar and God indicate that He was teaching separation of church and state?

Is there any reason to believe that angels do not procreate? Gen. 6:2; 2 Pet. 2:4; Jude 6.

Record your answer to these self-examination questions.

Should I ever turn away from those I witness to and offer the gospel invitation to others?

Why should I pay taxes?

Whom does God say I have to love? How well do I do it?

Respond to God in prayer and praise.

Pray for urgency in telling others to accept the invitation. Pray for understanding between things secular and things spiritual. Praise God that Jesus is Lord of all.

Matthew 23

Jesus denounces the Pharisees for their hypocrisy.

Read prayerfully the following sections.

Ch. 23:1–12	Jesus proclaims to the people the practices of the Pharisees.
Ch. 23:13–36	Jesus pronounces displeasure on the play-acting Pharisees.
Ch. 23:37–39	Jesus pleads with passion for Jerusalem.

Review the passage and answer these context questions.

What were the teachers of the Law not practicing?

How did the Pharisees appear to men? How did they appear to God?

When will the city of Jerusalem recognize Jesus?

Research study questions; refer to scripture cross-references.

What were the "heavy loads" that the Pharisees were placing on people's shoulders? Matt. 23:13; Luke 11:46.

Who is the only genuine teacher of the Law? What is the purpose of the Law? Why must the teaching of the Law begin at the cross? Gal. 3:23, 24.

The Pharisees were zealous and sincere. Was their devotion enough? Is. 1:10–20.

Record your answer to these self-examination questions.

Do my actions confirm what I believe and teach or do they contradict it?

How can I cultivate a more servant-like attitude?

How many opportunities have I had to commit my life to Christ?

Respond to God in prayer and praise.

Ask God to rid you of hypocrisy. Ask for guidance so we don't neglect justice, mercy, and faithfulness. Praise God for the promise of Christ's return.

Jesus predicts the fall of Jerusalem and the end of the age.

Read prayerfully the following sections.

Ch. 24:1–14	Jesus warns to watch out for rumors of wars in the last days.
Ch. 24:15–22	Jesus warns of troubling times in this tribulation period.
Ch. 24:23–51	Jesus warns that the day and hour of His return is unknown.

Review the passage and answer these context questions.

When will Jerusalem be destroyed?

When will Jesus return to earth again?

How will the Son of Man appear when He returns?

Research study questions; refer to scripture cross-references.

What will happen to the city of Jerusalem in the last days? Luke 21:20–24.

Where else are details of the establishment of false worship? Dan. 9:27; 11:31; 12:11; 2 Thess. 2:7–10.

What parables does Jesus teach to warn people to be alert? What will happen to those who are unbelievers? Matt. 24:42–51.

Record your answer to these self-examination questions.

How willing am I to witness for Jesus in time of persecution?

How can we counter doomsday deceivers?

What can I do to be more watchful and faithful as the "day of the Lord" approaches?

Respond to God in prayer and praise.

Ask for help not to be deceived by false christs. Praise God for His Word that does not pass away. Ask for help to remain faithful until the Lord returns.

Matthew 25

Parables of warning about Jesus' return and coming judgment.

Read prayerfully the following sections.

Ch. 25:1–13	Jesus tells a parable of the five wise and five foolish virgins.
Ch. 25:14–30	Jesus tells a parable of the profitable and unprofitable servants.
Ch. 25:31–46	Jesus tells of commendation for the sheep and condemnation for the goats.

Review the passage and answer these context questions.

Why should people be watching for Christ's return?

Who did the man with the one talent blame for his lack of preparedness?

How long will the punishment of the wicked last?

Research study questions; refer to scripture cross-references.

Who do you think the virgins, the friends of the bride, speak of? Rev. 19:7–9.

Jesus has gone on a journey (His ascension). What responsibilities do believers have in His absence? Matt. 28:19, 20. What rewards do faithful servants receive? 1 Cor. 3:12–15.

How do unbelievers treat God's people during tribulation times? Rev. 6:9–11.

Record your answer to these self-examination questions.

What preparations have I made for the return of Jesus?

How am I using the talents Jesus has given me?

How can I identify those in need?

Respond to God in prayer and praise.

Pray for a greater diligence in watching for the Lord's return. Pray for more wisdom to use what the Master has given. Praise God for the inheritance laid up in heaven.

Matthew 26:1–56

Jesus breaks bread with the disciples and is betrayed by Judas.

Read prayerfully the following sections.

Ch. 26:1–16	Jesus' body is anointed at Bethany for His burial.
Ch. 26:17–30	Jesus breaks bread with the disciples while Judas plans to betray Him.
Ch. 26:31–46	Jesus bows in prayer at Gethsemane while the disciples bed down.
Ch. 26:47–56	Jesus is betrayed by Judas, bound by soldiers, and abandoned by the disciples.

Review the passage and answer these context questions.

How did the chief priests plan to arrest Jesus?

Why were the disciples wrong in their judgment of this woman?

How many disciples promised Jesus that they would not disown Him?

Research study questions; refer to scripture cross-references.

Who was the woman who anointed Jesus? Who led the indignation about such waste? John 12:1–4.

What special responsibility was given to Judas? Who or what caused him to betray Jesus? John 12:6; Luke 22:3.

What do the following verses instruct about the Lord's Supper in the present day? 1 Cor. 11:23–33.

Record your answer to these self-examination questions.

What costly possession would I sacrifice for Jesus?

When was the last time I broke bread and received it as if it came directly from Jesus?

How prepared am I to defend Jesus even though it may appear foolish to some?

Respond to God in prayer and praise.

Ask for generosity in spirit in giving to Jesus. Ask for a thankful heart to remember Him. Praise God for the Savior's willingness to go to the cross.

Matthew 26:57–75

Jesus is arrested and brought before the chief priest.

Read prayerfully the following sections.

Ch. 26:57–68 Jesus is charged before Caiaphas and chief priests.
Ch. 26:69–75 Peter calls down curses as he casts off association with Jesus just as the rooster crows.

Review the passage and answer these context questions.

For what sort of evidence was the Sanhedrin searching?

What was Jesus' reply to the question; "Tell us if you are the Christ"?

How strong was Peter's denial of Jesus?

Research study questions; refer to scripture cross-references.

Jesus' second trial was before Caiaphas. What is known of His first trial and whom was it before? John 18:12–14.

Should Peter have followed Jesus at this time? In Peter's life there were several steps that led to his fall. What were these steps? What did Peter fail to do? Matt. 26:41.

What was the context of Jesus' statement, "Destroy this temple, and I will raise it again in three days"? John 2:19.

Record your answer to these self-examination questions.

What sort of witness am I, false or true?

How courageous am I when called to identify with Christ?

Have I disowned Christ in deed if not in word?

Respond to God in prayer and praise.

Praise God for the promise of Christ's return.
Pray for strength to give allegiance to Jesus at all times.

Matthew 27:1–26

Jesus is tried before the chief priests and Pilate and then prosecuted.

Read prayerfully the following sections.

Ch. 27:1–10	Judas is condemned, casts coins before the chief priests, and commits suicide.
Ch. 27:11–26	Chief priests convince crowd to ask for Barabbas and crucify Jesus.

Review the passage and answer these context questions.

How did Judas see Jesus after Jesus was condemned to death?

What caused Judas to commit suicide?

Why did the chief priests want Jesus put to death?

Research study questions; refer to scripture cross-references.

In Judas' case, feeling guilty did not bring salvation. What did Judas need to do? Luke 13:3, 5.

What did the Psalmist say about the place where Judas would be buried? Acts 1:20; Ps. 69:25.

Where did Pilate get the idea that if he washed his hands he would be free of guilt? Deut. 21:6–9.

Record your answer to these self-examination questions.

What actions of mine betray Christ before others?

How willing am I to stand firm and acknowledge Christ as King?

Have I confessed my sins to God and found freedom from guilt in Christ?

Respond to God in prayer and praise.

Ask for true repentance after sin and failure.
Pray for strength and courage to make right decisions.

Matthew 27:27–66

Jesus is mocked, crucified, and buried. The tomb is secured.

Read prayerfully the following sections.

Ch. 27:27–44	Jesus is mocked by soldiers, crowd, and chief priests, then crucified.
Ch. 27:45–56	Jesus cries out loud; the curtain is torn; and the centurion believes.
Ch. 27:57–61	A rich man clothes Christ's body and places it in a cut-out tomb.
Ch. 27:62–66	Chief priests enclose the tomb and cover it with a stone.

Review the passage and answer these context questions.

What did all of Jesus' mockers have in common?

Why had the women followed Jesus to the cross?

How well protected was the tomb of Jesus from body stealers?

Research study questions; refer to scripture cross-references.

What is the significance of the crown of thorns and the cross? Gen. 3:17, 18; Gal. 3:13.

Did Jesus quote all of Psalm 22 from the cross? Ps. 22; Is. 53.

What was the significance of the curtain being torn from top to bottom? Heb. 10:9–22.

Record your answer to these self-examination questions.

How willing am I to take up my cross and follow Jesus?

In what way am I watching and waiting to care for the needs of others?

What have I given to Jesus that I had prepared for myself?

Respond to God in prayer and praise.

**Praise God that Jesus suffered to save others.
Praise God the curtain has been removed. Pray for a heart to care for others.**

Matthew 28

Disciples thought Jesus was dead, but the tomb was empty.

Read prayerfully the following sections.

Ch. 28:1	Women arrive at the tomb thinking Jesus is dead.
Ch. 28:2–8	Angel announces that Jesus is alive and risen.
Ch. 28:9–15	Jesus sends the women to tell disciples.
Ch. 28:16–20	Jesus commissions disciples, assuring them of His power.

Review the passage and answer these context questions.

What did the women find when they came to the tomb?

Where did the Jews get their story that the disciples stole the body of Jesus?

What proves that the disciples had not manufactured the resurrection account?

Research study questions; refer to scripture cross-references.

Was the stone rolled away to let Jesus out or to let the disciples in? John 20:19.

Where did the disciples have to go to meet the risen Christ? How many times did Jesus make an appearance? 1 Cor. 15:1–6.

The guards distorted the message. What did the brave women do? Matt. 28:5–10.

Record your answer to these self-examination questions.

What is my position if I think Jesus is still dead?

When did I first hear the news that He was raised? How has it affected my life?

How responsible am I in carrying out the Great Commission?

Respond to God in prayer and praise.

Praise God that Jesus is raised from the dead. Ask for eyes of faith to see the risen Lord. Ask for greater help in obeying the Great Commission.

Mark 1

John the Baptist's ministry and Jesus' mission are told by Mark.

Read prayerfully the following sections.

Ch. 1:1–13	Christ's path is prepared, Jesus is baptized, and the Father is pleased.
Ch. 1:14–20	John is imprisoned; Jesus calls disciples to be fishers of men.
Ch. 1:21–34	Jesus pacifies a man; the people are amazed; and He heals many.
Ch. 1:35–45	Jesus prays alone, preaches in villages, and cleanses a leper.

Review the passage and answer these context questions.

What was the content of John the Baptist's message?

What was the content of Jesus' message?

The healed leper disobeyed Jesus, but with what result?

Research study questions; refer to scripture cross-references.

Who are the two Old Testament prophets that join Mark in declaring that Jesus is the Son of God? Is. 40:3; Mal. 3:1.

In what way was John the Baptist identified with Elijah? 2 Kgs. 1:8; Mal. 4:5.

In what two ways did the demon witness to Jesus' identity? Mark 1:24.

How do the following verses describe Jesus' relationship with His Father? Is. 50:4–9.

Record your answer to these self-examination questions.

How often do I want to exalt myself rather than Jesus?

In what way have I been called to become a "fisher of men"?

How has "the Holy One of God" healed me spiritually?

Respond to God in prayer and praise.

Praise God for ministering angels. Ask for more faith to follow the call of Christ. Praise God for the compassion of Jesus.

Mark 2

Jesus cures a paralytic, calls Levi, and is challenged by critics.

Read prayerfully the following sections.

Ch. 2:1–12	Jesus cures a paralyzed man, cleanses his sins, and is criticized.
Ch. 2:13–17	Jesus calls Levi and eats with tax collectors.
Ch. 2:18–2	Jesus is challenged by critics and compares the old covenant with the new.
Ch. 2:23–8	Jesus charges critics with confusion regarding the Sabbath.

Review the passage and answer these context questions.

What authority did Jesus the Son of man have?

Why did Jesus fellowship with tax collectors and sinners?

Who set the rules on Sabbath keeping?

Research study questions; refer to scripture cross-references.

Is all suffering and sickness caused by sin? What are some other causes? Job 1:8–10; Ps. 38; 2 Cor. 1:3–5; 12:7–10; 1 Pet. 1:6–8.

What new name did Jesus give to Levi? Matt. 9:9. Who are the only people Jesus can save? Luke 19:10.

The old covenant was to be replaced. What were the limitations in the old? Rom. 8:3; Heb. 8:13.

Record your answer to these self-examination questions.

How concerned am I about introducing others to Jesus?

How many non-Christians do I know?

In what way is my life new since trusting Christ?

Respond to God in prayer and praise.

Pray that others might have the faith to come to Jesus. Ask for more love to reach out and eat with those in need. Praise God for the newness of life Jesus brings.

Mark 3

Jesus is under scrutiny, subdues demons, and appoints the twelve.

Read prayerfully the following sections.

Ch. 3:1–6	Jesus worries the Pharisees by healing a withered hand.
Ch. 3:7–12	Jesus withdraws with His disciples while demons are wonderstruck.
Ch. 3:13–19	Jesus wants the disciples to be with Him, so He appoints twelve.
Ch. 3:20–35	Jesus is written off as the prince of demons by teachers of the Law.

Review the passage and answer these context questions.

What was Jesus' attitude to those who showed no compassion?

Whom did Jesus call to be His disciples?

Whom does Jesus name as His relatives?

Research study questions; refer to scripture cross-references.

What indicates that the Pharisees had more concern for their own well-being than for their fellow man? Luke 6:10; 13:15.

What were Jesus' credentials? Why didn't He need the demon's acknowledgement? Matt. 11:1–5.

Can a person resist the Holy Spirit? Matt. 12:32; John 16:8–12.

Record your answer to these self-examination questions.

When did I acknowledge Jesus as the Son of God?

What role does Jesus have for me as a disciple, and am I fulfilling it?

How does the Holy Spirit direct me and guide me?

Respond to God in prayer and praise.

Ask for faith to obey Jesus' command. Praise God for His power.
Pray for a greater desire to walk with Jesus.

Mark 4:1–34

Jesus speaks in parables—the sower, the lamp on a stand, and seeds.

Read prayerfully the following sections.

Ch. 4:1–20	Jesus speaks of a sower who sows seed in different soils.
Ch. 4:21–25	Jesus states that a light should not be covered but set on a stand.
Ch. 4:26–29	Jesus speaks of scattering seed and then discusses the stages to harvest.
Ch. 4:30–34	Jesus describes the unnatural growth of a mustard plant.

Review the passage and answer these context questions.

What forces are active when the Word of God is sown?

What is the application of the growing seed?

Where is the apparent contradiction in the parable of the mustard seed?

Research study questions; refer to scripture cross-references.

What must happen to the hard heart before it is ready to receive the Word of God? Jer. 4:3; Hos. 10:12.

What does Jesus ask His disciples to be in the world? Matt. 5:13–16.

What indicates that this parable of the mustard seed refers to unnatural growth? Matt. 13:32.

Record your answer to these self-examination questions.

What is my response to God's Word? What prevents it from taking root?

How am I using my gifts for God's service?

What is my responsibility in soul-winning?

Respond to God in prayer and praise.

Ask for a heart to respond to God's Word.
Ask for a life that shines for Jesus. Praise God for the wonders of nature.

Mark 4:35—5:43

Jesus calms storm, frees the demon possessed, and cures a suffering woman.

Read prayerfully the following sections.

Ch. 4:35–41	Jesus, unconcerned, is awakened; He chastises disciples and calms the storm.
Ch. 5:1–20	Jesus unchains man by casting demons into pigs.
Ch. 5:21–34	Woman, unnoticed, touches Jesus' clothes in crowd and is cured.
Ch. 5:35–43	Jesus, unmoved by the commotion of crowd, raises child to life.

Review the passage and answer these context questions.

Why did Jesus fall asleep in the boat?

Why did the people in the area plead with Jesus to leave?

Why would this woman be afraid in the presence of the Healer?

Research study questions; refer to scripture cross-references.

The disciples were in a storm because of their obedience. What Old Testament character was in a storm because of his disobedience? What lesson can be learned from this? Jonah 1—3.

What are some indications that demons believe in God, prayer, and the hereafter? Mark 5:7; Matt. 8:29; Jam. 2:19.

Where will our spirit go when we die? Eccl. 12:7; 1 Thess. 4:14.

Record your answer to these self-examination questions.

In what way can I exercise faith in the storms of life?

When did I tell members of my family that I became a Christian?

How can I show faith in suffering?

Respond to God in prayer and praise.

Pray for peace in the storms of life. Ask to be set free from sins that trap you. Pray for a daily touch from Jesus.

Mark 6

Disciples are sent; John is beheaded; thousands are fed; and Jesus walks on water.

Read prayerfully the following sections.

Ch. 6:1–13	Jesus offends because of family background; the disciples are commissioned to preach.
Ch. 6:14–29	Herod fears John, but at a feast his family plots John's fate.
Ch. 6:30–44	Jesus feeds five thousand with five loaves and two fishes.
Ch. 6:45–56	Jesus, walking on the water, confronts disciples and calms their fears.

Review the passage and answer these context questions.

Why could Jesus not perform many miracles in His hometown?

Why did Herod think that John had risen from the dead?

What had the disciples not understood about the loaves?

Research study questions; refer to scripture cross-references.

What was the attitude of the hometown folk on Jesus' first visit? Luke 4:16–30. Was there any difference this time?

Why did Jesus send the disciples two by two? Eccl. 4:9–12. Were the disciples always successful in their mission? Matt. 17:14–21.

Is it possible that Mark wrote his Gospel as Peter's scribe? Would this explain Mark's omission of the rest of the storm account? Matt. 14:22–36.

Record your answer to these self-examination questions.

What sort of welcome and fellowship do I give to local preachers?

How do I allow myself to be compromised by rash promises and family ties?

How long has it taken me to realize that little is much in the Lord's hands?

Respond to God in prayer and praise.

Ask for more opportunities to help the Lord's servants. Praise God for the quiet place of rest. Ask for more courage and peace in the storms of life.

Mark

7

Jesus rebukes Pharisees, heals woman and deaf-mute man.

Read prayerfully the following sections.

Ch. 7:1–23	Jesus contradicts Pharisees' argument that His disciples are lawbreakers.
Ch. 7:24–30	Jesus hears the cry of the Canaanite woman and cures her child.
Ch. 7:31–37	Jesus calls aside the deaf mute, cures him, and then commands silence.

Review the passage and answer these context questions.

What did the Pharisees lack in their worship?

How do traditions fit in with the Word of God?

What impressed Jesus about the Gentile woman's reply?

Research study questions; refer to scripture cross-references.

Part of the Pharisees' tradition was to will their wealth to the temple and thus excuse themselves from family responsibilities. What are our responsibilities toward our aging parents? Deut. 5:16; 27:16; 1 Tim. 5:8.

Which woman showed good knowledge as well as faith to agree that the Jews had first claim on Jesus? John 4:1–27.

Knowing that the man was deaf, was this the reason Jesus used touch to heal him? Mark 7:33–35.

Record your answer to these self-examination questions.

When do traditions take the place of the Bible in my beliefs?

How willing am I to believe that Jesus hears the cry of all who come to Him?

How much do I care for my friends? Would I beg Jesus to save them?

Respond to God in prayer and praise.

Pray for wisdom to discern what is important and unimportant.
Praise God that His salvation is offered to all. Pray for true recognition of Jesus' power.

Mark 8

Jesus shows compassion, gives a warning, touches the blind, and predicts His death.

Read prayerfully the following sections.

Ch. 8:1–13	Jesus cares for the hungry, then condemns Pharisees for seeking signs.
Ch. 8:14–21	Jesus cautions His disciples to be careful of the yeast of the Pharisees.
Ch. 8:22–26	Jesus cures a blind man's cataracts so that he can see clearly.
Ch. 8:27–38	Peter confesses Christ, and Jesus predicts His death and resurrection.

Review the passage and answer these context questions.

Why was Jesus exasperated at the Pharisees' request for a sign?

Why was Jesus exasperated at the disciples' lack of understanding?

What is the answer to the question Jesus asks in verse 37?

Research study questions; refer to scripture cross-references.

The disciples had forgotten it was the same Jesus who had fed the multitudes. What scripture should remind Christians that Jesus never changes? Heb. 13:8.

What does "yeast" or "leaven" refer to in the Bible? Ex. 12:18–20; 23:18; 34:25; Lev. 2:11.

Why is it important to acknowledge Jesus Christ as Lord and Savior? John 8:19–24; Rom. 10:9, 10; 1 Cor. 12:1–3; 1 John 2:22–27; 4:1–3.

Record your answer to these self-examination questions.

Why would I rather have a "sign" than trust in God's Word?

When have I trusted God by faith for the outcome to my problems?

How has God touched me and enabled me to see even more clearly?

Respond to God in prayer and praise.

Pray for a greater compassion for the hungry.
Ask for more wisdom to understand spiritual things. Praise God for opening blinded eyes.

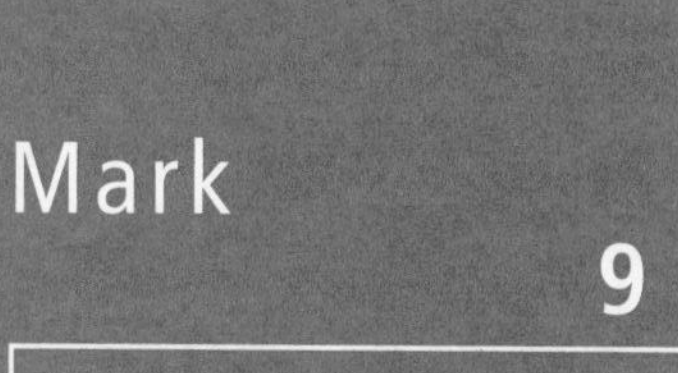

Jesus is transfigured; a demon withstood; and the disciples and sectarianism are rebuked.

Read prayerfully the following sections.

Ch. 9:1–13	Jesus is transfigured before three disciples and talks to Moses and Elijah.
Ch. 9:14–32	Jesus transforms the possessed and teaches the disciples.
Ch. 9:33–41	Jesus teaches the disciples about teamwork and taking stock before they judge.
Ch. 9:42–50	Jesus tutors disciples on the importance of avoiding evil.

Review the passage and answer these context questions.

Who were the disciples that saw Jesus clothed in His kingdom glory?

Why were the people filled with wonder when Jesus descended?

In the closing verses, what caused Jesus to warn His disciples?

Research study questions; refer to scripture cross-references.

What happened to Elijah's body when he departed from this earth? What do we read about Moses' body? 2 Kgs. 2:11; Deut. 34:5, 6; Jude 1:8, 9.

Why had the disciples failed to cast out the demon? Mark 9:29.

Jesus mentions hell fourteen times more often than heaven. How long does hell last? Rev. 20:10.

Record your answer to these self-examination questions.

How do I listen to what Jesus is saying? How can I give Him my full attention?

What can I pray to overcome my disbelief?

How can I have a servant's heart? How often does my pride prevent this?

Respond to God in prayer and praise.

Praise God for His Son from heaven.
Ask for more faith to believe the impossible. Pray for true humility.

Jesus is challenged on divorce, children, riches, and position, then He heals Bartimaeus.

Read prayerfully the following sections.

Ch. 10:1–12	Jesus is challenged on Moses' policy on divorce.
Ch. 10:13–16	Jesus calls children for the kingdom of heaven.
Ch. 10:17–31	Jesus cites commandments to rich ruler who want to cling to wealth.
Ch. 10:32–52	Jesus chides James and John for contending about position.

Review the passage and answer these context questions.

Why did Jesus say that the Law allowed divorce?

What hindered the rich young ruler from following Jesus?

What is Jesus' teaching on greatness?

How precise was the blind man's answer to Jesus?

Research study questions; refer to scripture cross-references.

Because marriage is a physical union, should the only reason for dissolution be death? Matt. 5:32; 19:19; Rom. 7:1–3.

How can one know that keeping the Law cannot save us? Gal. 2:16–21; Eph. 2:8–10.

Who was the only other person in the Gospels who called Jesus "Rabbi"? John 20:16.

Record your answer to these self-examination questions.

How willing am I to make an unconditional commitment to the person I marry?

In what way am I seeking to win children for heaven?

If God calls me into leadership, how willing am I to serve others?

Respond to God in prayer and praise.

Ask for help and understanding when faced with difficulty.
Praise God that children can come to Him. Pray for more obedience to follow, whatever the cost.

Mark 11

Jesus enters Jerusalem, transforms the temple, and smites the fig tree.

Read prayerfully the following sections.

Ch. 11:1–11	Jesus is carried on a donkey as crowds cover the road with cloaks.
Ch. 11:12–19	Jesus casts corrupt moneychangers out of the temple.
Ch. 11:20–26	Jesus charges disciples to unconditionally forgive others.
Ch. 11:27–33	Jesus is cross-examined by chief priests in the temple.

Review the passage and answer these context questions.

What simple incident reveals God is in control of events?

Who had turned the temple into "a den of robbers"?

What hinders forgiveness?

Research study questions; refer to scripture cross-references.

What messianic prophecy was Jesus fulfilling by riding into Jerusalem on a donkey? Zech. 9:9.

What scriptures did Jesus use to justify His cleansing of the temple? Is. 56:7; Jer. 7:11.

How did Jesus show the chief priests that He was wiser than Solomon?

Record your answer to these self-examination questions.

How willing am I to do the Lord's bidding without question?

Why should I forgive those who have wronged me? What's in it for me?

What convinces me that I need no other authority but God's to do His work?

Respond to God in prayer and praise.

Remember the Lord is great and worthy to be praised.
Ask for a heart cleansed from sin. Pray for the grace to forgive others.
Pray for a spirit of trust so as not to question God inappropriately.

Parable on tenants; Jesus is challenged on taxes, resurrection, and teachings.

Read prayerfully the following sections.

Ch. 12:1–12	Jesus teaches the parable of the tenants.
Ch. 12:13–17	Teachers try to trick Jesus on the subject of taxes.
Ch. 12:18–40	Sadducees test Jesus on the resurrection and the commandments.
Ch. 12:41–44	Jesus teaches His disciples a lesson on true giving.

Review the passage and answer these context questions.

How did the parable of the tenants apply to the leaders of Israel?

What was the hypocrisy that Jesus saw?

How specific is this passage on the procreation of angels?

Research study questions; refer to scripture cross-references.

Where in the Bible is the scripture Jesus was referring to in verse 10?

On the subject of angels, does this passage state, as many hold, that angels are sexless beings? Or does it simply say that, in a place of perfection, there is no need for the institution of marriage? Mark 12:25.

What do the following scriptures teach about ritual? 1 Sam. 15:22; Ps. 51:16, 17; 141:1, 2.

Record your answer to these self-examination questions.

How do I treat God's appointees—with honor and respect or otherwise?

How often am I critical when God is using others?

How much do I love my neighbor—how much do I love myself?

Respond to God in prayer and praise.

Ask for more diligence in being a good steward. Pray for wisdom in dealing with the details of life. Praise God for the prospect of a perfect life in heaven.

Mark 13

Jesus claims that prophecies will be fulfilled.

Read prayerfully the following sections.

Ch. 13:1–13	Jesus warns of rumors of wars and hatred of men in the end time.
Ch. 13:14–23	Jesus warns against false witnesses and deceivers in the last days.
Ch. 13:24–37	Jesus warns about worsening conditions before His return.

Review the passage and answer these context questions.

What question did the disciples ask Jesus?

In context, what does this "generation" mean? Does it mean this unbelieving Jewish nation?

What are the "four watches" mentioned as possibilities of the time when Christ might return?

Research study questions; refer to scripture cross-references.

What do we read in the New Testament about false prophets of the end times? Matt. 7:14–29; Acts 20:28–31; 1 John 4:1–6.

What will the false messiah do before Jesus returns? 2 Thess. 2:1–12; Rev. 13:11–18.

What parables does Jesus teach to warn people to be alert? Matt. 13.

Record your answer to these self-examination questions.

How can I stand firm as I witness for Jesus in time of persecution?

What is our argument against doomsday deceivers?

What must I do to be watchful and faithful as the day of the Lord approaches?

Respond to God in prayer and praise.

Pray for a prepared heart to wait for the Lord's return. Praise God that Jesus is coming. Ask for alertness in looking for the signs of His coming.

Mark 14:1–52

Jesus anointed at Bethany, betrayed by Judas, and breaks bread with disciples.

Read prayerfully the following sections.

Ch. 14:1–10	Woman breaks a jar of ointment and anoints Jesus.
Ch. 14:11–26	Jesus breaks bread with disciples while Judas plans betrayal.
Ch. 14:27–42	Jesus bows in Gethsemane while His followers bed down.
Ch. 14:43–52	Jesus betrayed, is bound by soldiers, and abandoned by disciples.

Review the passage and answer these context questions.

Why was Jesus so appreciative of this woman's action?

What words did Judas offer at the Passover supper?

How seriously did the disciples take the threat of danger in the garden?

Research study questions; refer to scripture cross-references.

Who was the woman who anointed Jesus? What extra information is given in John? John 12:1–3.

Who and what caused Judas to betray Jesus? John 12:4; 13:27.

What do the following verses teach regarding the observance of the Lord's Supper? 1 Cor. 11:23–33.

Record your answer to these self-examination questions.

How do I make preparation regularly to remember the Lord?

How often do I go to sleep when praying? What can I change to be more faithful?

Like Peter, in what ways do I sometimes act foolishly in the defense of Christ?

Respond to God in prayer and praise.

Ask for a true heart of love toward Jesus. Pray for more opportunities to partake of the Lord's Supper. Praise God for the victory in Gethsemane's garden.

Mark 14:53—15:15

Jesus is arrested, disowned, and tried before priests and Pilate, then prosecuted.

Read prayerfully the following sections.

Ch. 14:53–65	Jesus is captured and brought before chief priests to be charged.
Ch. 14:66–72	Peter curses as he casts off Jesus and the cock crows.
Ch. 15:1–15	Jesus consigned to Pilate while chief priests persuade crowd.

Review the passage and answer these context questions.

How many testified falsely against Jesus?

What questions were asked that led Peter to deny Jesus?

What was the answer to Pilate's question, "What crime has He committed?"

Research study questions; refer to scripture cross-references.

Jesus' Jewish and Roman trials were conducted in three stages. Identify two of the stages in Mark's Gospel. What is known regarding the first stage? John 18:13–24

Should Peter have been following Jesus at this time? There were several stages in Peter's fall. What were they? Matt. 26:40; Luke 22:33.

What can be concluded from Pilate's repeated statement that he found no fault in Jesus? Matt. 27:24; Luke 23:14, 22; John 18:38; 19:4, 14.

Record your answer to these self-examination questions.

Whose example should I follow when I am asked questions that make no sense?

When have I denied Jesus either in word or by my silence?

How willing am I to stand firm and acknowledge Christ as King?

Respond to God in prayer and praise.

Ask for wisdom to know when not to speak.
Praise God that Jesus is now seated in heaven. Ask for watchfulness against entrapment.

Mark 15:16–47

Jesus is scoffed at, crucified, buried, and sealed in a tomb.

Read prayerfully the following sections.

Ch. 15:16–20	Soldiers scoff at Jesus, striking Him with a staff and spitting on Him.
Ch. 15:21–32	Simon ordered to carry the cross; scoffers scorn Jesus.
Ch. 15:33–47	Jesus cries out loud while centurion states "this is the Son of God".

Review the passage and answer these context questions.

What was "hurled" at Jesus as He hung on the cross?

What caused the centurion to believe?

How closely did the women follow Jesus even after His death?

Research study questions; refer to scripture cross-references.

What prophecy was fulfilled by the action of the soldiers when they cast lots for Jesus' clothes? Ps. 22:18.

What were the two remarkable events that took place at Jesus' death? Matt. 27:51; Heb. 10:12–22.

Who assisted Joseph of Arimathea in the burial of Jesus? John 19:38, 39.

Record your answer to these self-examination questions.

How do I view Jesus—as someone to blaspheme or someone to worship?

When have my thoughtless words caused pain to others?

When or at what stage of my life did I acknowledge Jesus as the Son of God?

Respond to God in prayer and praise.

Praise God that Jesus suffered and died for you.
Pray for a willingness to bear the cross. Praise God for the torn curtain.

Mark 16

Jesus is raised, appears to women, and commissions the disciples.

Read prayerfully the following sections.

Ch. 16:1–8	Women survey the tomb, finding the stone swept away and Jesus absent.
Ch. 16:9–11	Women speak to mourners and say, "Jesus is risen".
Ch. 16:12–14	Jesus is seen on several occasions by stubborn, skeptical disciples.
Ch. 16:15–20	Jesus assigns disciples to spread the gospel and then ascends.

Review the passage and answer these context questions.

What emotions were expressed at the tomb?

Why did Jesus have to rebuke His disciples after His resurrection?

What footnote is added regarding verses 9 to 20?

Research study questions; refer to scripture cross-references.

Why is the doctrine of the resurrection one of the most important in the Christian faith? 1 Cor. 15:1–8.

Miracles were given as special credentials to certain individuals to prove that they came from God. Who were the other individuals? Ex. 4:1–9; 2 Kgs. 2:14–25.

Is it wise to drink poison or pick up a snake to prove one's faith in God? What was Jesus' attitude when the devil asked Him to put Himself in danger? Matt. 4:4–7.

Record your answer to these self-examination questions.

How willing am I to begin a mission knowing there are difficulties ahead?

How often am I absent from the place where God speaks?

How is my Christian life and growth affected by my unbelief?

Respond to God in prayer and praise.

Praise God that the stone has been rolled away.
Ask for boldness to declare that Christ is risen. Ask for faith in the midst of unbelief.

Luke 1

The births of John and Jesus are foretold, and parents glorify God.

Read prayerfully the following sections.

Ch. 1:1–25	The birth of John the Baptist is foretold by an angel to Zechariah.
Ch. 1:26–38	The birth of Jesus is foretold to Mary by the angel Gabriel.
Ch. 1:39–56	Elizabeth blesses Mary and glorifies the Lord God, her Savior.
Ch. 1:57–80	John is born, and his father Zechariah praises the God of Israel.

Review the passage and answer these context questions.

How did Luke go about writing this Gospel?

What was the angel's answer to Mary when she stated that she was a virgin?

What was the mission of John?

Research study questions; refer to scripture cross-references.

Zechariah is instructed to dedicate John to God to be a Nazarite. What did this entail? Num. 6:1–21.

From the message of the angel to Mary what is learned about the humanity and deity of Jesus Christ? Luke 1:32–35.

How many things does Mary recall that God has done for her? What promises was God fulfilling to Israel? Gen. 12:1–3; 22:18; 26:4; 28:14; Ps. 98:1–3; Is. 9:6.

Record your answer to these self-examination questions.

How does my lack of faith stop others from hearing the message of God?

When God speaks to me, how willing am I to obey?

How often do I praise God for the things He has done for me?

Respond to God in prayer and praise.

Praise God for answered prayer.
Pray for a heart to obey when God directs. Ask for words to sing His praises.

www.SimplyCharlotteMason.com

Luke 2

Jesus is born and adored by angels, shepherds, Simeon, and Anna.

Read prayerfully the following sections.

Ch. 2:1–20	Jesus is born; angels declare His birth while shepherds break camp.
Ch. 2:21–40	Jesus brings blessing to Simeon and Anna, who prophesy.
Ch. 2:41–52	Jesus is brought to the temple and stays for a while on His Father's business.

Review the passage and answer these context questions.

What do we learn here about God's attitude toward men?

How satisfied was Simeon on seeing Jesus?

What sort of conversation did Jesus have with the teachers in the temple?

Research study questions; refer to scripture cross-references.

Could the angels have been as amazed as the shepherds at the thought that God the Son had become a helpless babe? 2 Cor. 8:9; 1 Tim. 3:16.

Simeon's song of praise is the fifth and last recorded by Luke. What can be learned from the others? Luke 1:42–45; 46–56; 67–79; 2:13, 14.

What did Simeon prophesy to Mary and when did the prophecy begin? Luke 2:34, 35.

Record your answer to these self-examination questions.

How much room do I have in my life for Jesus?

How well do I understand the prophecies of Jesus' birth?

What time do I give to God? Who takes first place in my life?

Respond to God in prayer and praise.

Pray that others will make room for Jesus.
Offer glory to God. Pray for a greater desire to be about our Father's business.

John the Baptist ministers to many and Jesus' genealogy is given.

Read prayerfully the following sections.

Ch. 3:1–11	John declares the coming of the Messiah and preaches repentance.
Ch. 3:12–20	John denounces the actions of many and is imprisoned by Herod.
Ch. 3:21–22	Jesus is baptized by John and acclaimed by God.
Ch. 3:23–38	Adam's descendants are accounted for in the genealogy of Jesus.

Review the passage and answer these context questions.

What emphasis did Luke put on the ancestry of John?

What emphasis did Luke put on the ancestry of Jesus?

What emphasis did God the Father put on the ancestry of Jesus?

Research study questions; refer to scripture cross-references.

Whom did John resemble as he came preaching and baptizing? Luke 1:17; Matt. 3:4; 2 Kgs. 1:8.

Why did John describe self-righteous sinners as a "brood of vipers"? Matt. 23:31–33; John 8:44, 45.

Why did Jesus begin His ministry by being baptized? Matt. 3:15. On what other two occasions in the life of Jesus did God speak from heaven? Luke 9:32–36; John 12:28.

Record your answer to these self-examination questions.

How prepared am I to repent of my sin and come for cleansing?

What does God expect my attitude toward others to be?

How does God see me when I surrender to his will?

Respond to God in prayer and praise.

Pray for true repentance from sin. Praise God for John's faithfulness.
Pray for a desire to be obedient in baptism.

Luke 4

Jesus is tempted, and then rejected; He teaches with authority and heals many.

Read prayerfully the following sections.

Ch. 4:1–13	Jesus fasts for forty days and gains victory over Satan's temptations.
Ch. 4:14–30	Jesus infuriates crowd by reading from Isaiah, fulfilling prophecy.
Ch. 4:31–37	Jesus forces demon from man, and the audience is fascinated.
Ch. 4:38–44	Jesus heals Simon's mother in law, and many follow Him.

Review the passage and answer these context questions.

Jesus was filled with the Word of God and what else?

What else does this chapter say regarding Jesus and the Spirit?

Who did demons say Jesus is?

Research study questions; refer to scripture cross-references.

What would have happened to our situation as fallen creatures if Jesus had accepted Satan's offer of instant reign over the kingdoms of this world? 1 Cor. 15:12–19; Rev. 11:15.

As Jesus read from Isaiah, did the rabbis understand that He was claiming to be the Messiah? Is. 61:1, 2; Luke 4:28, 29.

How do demons acknowledge God according to James? Jam. 2:19.

Record your answer to these self-examination questions.

What is my biggest temptation, and how can I use scripture to overcome it?

How should I react when people reject the gospel message?

When my personal demons confront me, how can I obtain victory?

Respond to God in prayer and praise.

Ask for victory to overcome temptation. Praise God for the fulfillment of prophecy. Ask for greater assurance that God is able.

Jesus shows His power in fishing, healing, calling, and teaching.

Read prayerfully the following sections.

Ch. 5:1–11	Jesus commands disciples to cast for fish—later they will catch men.
Ch. 5:12–26	Jesus cures leper and commends faith of paralytic's friends.
Ch. 5:27–32	Jesus calls Levi, a tax collector, and then calls sinners to repentance.
Ch. 5:33–39	Jesus challenges Pharisees by comparing old covenant with new.

Review the passage and answer these context questions.

What two things were commendable in Peter at this time?

What troubled the Pharisees about Jesus?

Whom did Jesus come to save?

Research study questions; refer to scripture cross-references.

How many of Jesus' disciples were fishermen? What qualifications would fishermen have that would make them good disciples? Matt. 5:18–20.

What other person went to "great heights" to see Jesus? Luke 19:1–4. Why did the Pharisees think it was blasphemy for Jesus to tell the sick man that his sins were forgiven? Luke 5:21.

What does the parable of the wineskins teach about the old religion of Judaism? Heb. 8:13.

Record your answer to these self-examination questions.

When I fear that my Christian work is going nowhere, how does God help?

How much effort am I making to bring others to know Jesus' saving grace?

How do old traditions prevent us from accepting salvation by faith?

Respond to God in prayer and praise.

Pray for help in leading others to Christ. Praise God the Father for the Savior of sinners, Jesus Christ. Ask for a greater understanding of Jesus' teaching.

Luke 6

Jesus' ministry grows as He heals, teaches, and calls disciples.

Read prayerfully the following sections.

Ch. 6:1–11	Jesus heals on the Sabbath, citing an example of David to objecting Pharisees.
Ch. 6:12–19	Jesus humbles Himself before His Father before handpicking disciples.
Ch. 6:20–42	Luke's account of the Sermon on the Mount.
Ch. 6:43–49	Jesus highlights the danger of poor foundations.

Review the passage and answer these context questions.

Who determined whether the disciples were breaking the Law?

Whom does Jesus say we should seek to help?

When can we be sure that right and just words come from our mouths?

Research study questions; refer to scripture cross-references.

What is the difference between the Jewish Sabbath and the Christian Sunday? Does it cause confusion in Christian circles to call Sunday "the Sabbath," as one reflects keeping the Law while the other reflects commemoration and grace? Ex. 20:8–11; Acts 20:7; Rom. 14:1–15; 1 Cor. 16:1, 2.

Did Jesus know when He chose Judas Iscariot that Judas would betray Him? John 6:64.

How can the Sermon on the Mount be applied today?

Record your answer to these self-examination questions.

How quick am I to judge other people's actions while doing nothing myself?

In what way has my coming into contact with Jesus Christ healed me?

How does God expect me to act toward my enemies?

Respond to God in prayer and praise.

Ask for help to do good and not evil.
Ask for a greater determination to spend time alone in prayer. Praise God for His many blessings.

Luke 7

Jesus heals centurion's servant, raises widow's son, and is anointed by sinful woman.

Read prayerfully the following sections.

Ch. 7:1–10	Jesus commends centurion's faith and cures his servant.
Ch. 7:11–17	Jesus brings a widow's only son to life.
Ch. 7:18–35	Jesus confirms to John's disciples that He is the Messiah.
Ch. 7:36–50	Jesus compliments the woman who washed His feet with her tears.

Review the passage and answer these context questions.

Which of the centurion's virtues did Jesus find commendable?

From Jesus' answer to John the Baptist's query, what can we conclude was the purpose of miracles?

Whose example should we follow when it comes to devotion?

Research study questions; refer to scripture cross-references.

What can we learn from the other recorded occasion when Jesus marveled at the faith of a Gentile? Matt. 15:28.

How did Jesus face the greatest enemy that humankind will ever encounter? Heb. 2:14, 15.

Whose sin is Jesus able to forgive? Why did others on this occasion not receive forgiveness? Luke 7:49, 50; Acts 16:31; 2 Cor. 5:21.

Record your answer to these self-examination questions.

What attitude do I show when Jesus comes to answer my cry for help?

How can I help others in their hour of crisis?

In what way am I showing the truth to those who are in doubt?

Respond to God in prayer and praise.

Ask for more love for the nation and the church.
Ask for ears to hear Jesus say, "Don't cry." Ask for help not to backslide.

Luke 8

Jesus preaches, heals, and relates the parables of the sower and the candle.

Read prayerfully the following sections.

Ch. 8:1–15	Jesus speaks of a sower who sows seed in different soils.
Ch. 8:16–18	Jesus states that a light is not meant to be hidden.
Ch. 8:19–21	Jesus shows no partiality toward His own family.
Ch. 8:22–56	Jesus stills storm, unshackles possessed, heals suffering woman, and raises dead girl.

Review the passage and answer these context questions.

What was the ministry of women who followed Jesus?

What reward is there for listening when the Word is spoken?

How did Jesus place His mother and brothers in the over-all picture of God's kingdom?

Research study questions; refer to scripture cross-references.

How does faith come? Should all believers produce some sort of good fruit? Rom. 10:17. What are some of the fruits that can be produced? Matt. 13:8; Rom. 1:13; 15:25–28; Gal. 5:22; Col. 1:10; Heb. 13:15.

What church did Paul commend for living out Christianity before others? 1 Thess. 1:5–8.

Do demons believe in God? Jam. 2:19. What were some of the illnesses that demons seemed to produce? Matt. 12:22; Mark 1:26; 5:15; 9:17.

Record your answer to these self-examination questions.

When my faith is challenged, how firm is its foundation?

In what way am I letting my light shine before those who are in darkness?

How do I act or react when the storms of life strike?

Respond to God in prayer and praise.

Ask for a receptive heart to the Word of God.
Ask for a desire to let the Light shine. Praise God that He is impartial.

Luke 9

Jesus commissions followers, feeds five thousand, and is transfigured.

Read prayerfully the following sections.

Ch. 9:1–9	Jesus commissions twelve to communicate about the coming Kingdom.
Ch. 9:10–27	Disciples cater to thousands, and Jesus confirms Peter's confession.
Ch. 9:28–36	Jesus' clothes become clear as light, and a cloud engulfs them.
Ch. 9:37–62	Jesus cures child with convulsions, then cautions on pride.

Review the passage and answer these context questions.

How do we know that the disciples made a great impact?

What is the most valuable thing in the world?

What did Moses and Elijah speak to Jesus about?

Research study questions; refer to scripture cross-references.

Do miracles prove God's presence? Matt. 24:24; 2 Cor. 11:13–15; 2 Thess. 2:9, 10. What is the scriptural method today of testing true and false teaching? 1 John 2:18–29; 4:1–6.

Which disciples are named in the episode of the feeding of the five thousand, and who provided the loaves and fishes? John 6:6–9.

Was this a glimpse of the Lord's glorified body on the Mount of Transfiguration? Matt. 17:2; Rev. 1:12–16.

Record your answer to these self-examination questions.

In what way am I trusting God for material needs when called to serve?

How long has it taken me to realize that little "is much" in the Lord's hands?

How has God changed my life? Is it visible to others?

Respond to God in prayer and praise.

Ask for words to communicate the gospel.
Ask for bread to feed the multitude. Praise God for the glory of Jesus.

Luke 10

Jesus sends out disciples, teaches on the Good Samaritan, and rebukes Martha.

Read prayerfully the following sections.

Ch. 10:1–16	Jesus sends out seventy-two disciples, instructing them in their assignment.
Ch. 10:17–24	Disciples return and Jesus reveals Satan's stronghold has fallen.
Ch. 10:25–37	Jesus sketches story of the Good Samaritan.
Ch. 10:38–42	Jesus sings Mary's praise while her sister Martha serves.

Review the passage and answer these context questions.

In what were the disciples to rejoice?

What question was asked Jesus?

How did too much housework affect Martha?

Research study questions; refer to scripture cross-references.

What do the following scriptures say about the three ancient cities mentioned by Jesus? Gen. 19; Is. 23; Ezek. 26—28.

How can victory be claimed over the forces of evil today? Col. 2:15.

What did the Law teach about whom God's people should be showing mercy to? Ex. 23:4, 5; Micah 6:8.

Record your answer to these self-examination questions.

How am I trusting God for my provisions? What hinders me from serving Him fully?

How often do I help those who don't need help and neglect those who do?

When life gets too busy, am I finding rest in God's Word?

Respond to God in prayer and praise.

Ask for more grace to follow God's instructions.
Praise God that Jesus conquered Satan. Ask for more compassion for those in need.

Jesus teaches on prayer, demonic activity, miraculous signs, and hypocrisy.

Read prayerfully the following sections.

Ch. 11:1–13	Jesus coaches the disciples on prayer and gives an example.
Ch. 11:14–28	Jesus is charged with casting out demons by Beelzebub.
Ch. 11:29–36	Jesus compares Jonah's generation with the present unrepentant one.
Ch. 11:37–54	Jesus condemns the Pharisees' hypocritical practices.

Review the passage and answer these context questions.

What gift does the father give to those who ask?

How did Jesus drive out demons?

In their zeal for outward ritual, what had the Pharisees forgotten?

Research study questions; refer to scripture cross-references.

Can believers be assured that they have been forgiven if they cannot forgive others? Matt. 18:21–35; 1 John 3:8–10.

How did Jesus invade Satan's stronghold and destroy his armor and weapons? John 12:31–33.

What is the sign of Jonah? Will these Pharisees witness this sign? Matt.12:40; Acts 1:22; 3:15; 5:30–32.

Record your answer to these self-examination questions.

How persistent am I in prayer?

What is my defense when wrongly accused?

How is my personal legalism hindering others from coming to know Jesus?

Respond to God in prayer and praise.

Praise God that He hears prayer.
Ask for more help to obey when we hear God speak.
Ask for mercy for an unrepentant generation. Ask for wisdom to withstand legalism.

Luke 12

Jesus warns the disciples about worry and wealth and predicts His return.

Read prayerfully the following sections.

Ch. 12:1–12	Jesus warns to be aware of hypocrites and to trust in God's provision.
Ch. 12:13–21	Jesus weighs the danger of amassing worldly wealth.
Ch. 12:22–34	Jesus writes off any profit there is in worry, for God supplies needs.
Ch. 12:35–59	Jesus wills His people to be watchful and ready for His return.

Review the passage and answer these context questions.

When will the Holy Spirit teach us what to say?

In the parable of the rich fool, what sin is addressed?

What sort of treasure does Jesus offer?

Which servants are rewarded when the master returns?

Research study questions; refer to scripture cross-references.

How does leaven in the Scriptures symbolize sin? Ex. 12:15–20; 1 Cor. 5:6–8; Gal. 5:9.

What are the dangers of prosperity? Matt. 13:22; Prov. 30:7–9. How much will people leave behind when they depart this life? Ps. 39:5, 6; 1 Tim. 6:6–10, 17, 19.

How much longer do people live when they worry? Where does the Bible say a person should cast their cares? Ps. 55:22.

Record your answer to these self-examination questions.

When the entire world is against me, where can I place my confidence?

What is more important to me: material wealth or heavenly blessings?

How am I trusting God for the details of life?

Respond to God in prayer and praise.

Ask for trust that the Lord will provide. Ask for a greater awareness of the dangers of wealth. Praise God for the care He has for His children.

Jesus teaches in parables, heals a cripple, and describes God's kingdom.

Read prayerfully the following sections.

Ch. 13:1–9	Jesus calls for repentance through the parable of a fruitless fig tree.
Ch. 13:10–17	Jesus cures a cripple woman on the Sabbath, inducing a Pharisaical challenge.
Ch. 13:18–21	Jesus compares the kingdom to a mustard seed and to yeast.
Ch. 13:22–35	On His way to Jerusalem, Jesus offers the criteria for entering the kingdom.

Review the passage and answer these context questions.

What will happen to those who refuse to repent?

Who had caused the crippled woman's infirmity?

What effort should be made to find the way of salvation?

Research study questions; refer to scripture cross-references.

Why did Jesus move from the politically-charged question about the Galileans and Pilate? What was the more important subject that Jesus was concerned about? Luke 13:5.

In the parable a mustard seed produces a shrub as large as a tree. What institution might Jesus have been referring to?

When will the last sentence of chapter thirteen be fulfilled?
Matt. 24:30, 31; Zech. 12:10; 14:4.

Record your answer to these self-examination questions.

How many opportunities has God given me to repent and come to Him?

How often do I take the opportunity to praise God for His mercy and deliverance?

What small bad habit of mine could spread and affect the whole church?

Respond to God in prayer and praise.

Ask for help to truly repent. Praise God for the deliverance Jesus brings. Ask for more help to grow spiritually.

Luke 14

Jesus teaches parables on humility, indifference, and sacrifice.

Read prayerfully the following sections.

Ch. 14:1–6	Jesus challenges Pharisees when He cures suffering man on the Sabbath.
Ch. 14:7–14	Jesus calls dinner guests to be considerate concerning seating.
Ch. 14:15–24	Jesus cites parable of a man whose contemptuous guests were replaced.
Ch. 14:25–35	Jesus recounts parables that catalogue the cost of following Him.

Review the passage and answer these context questions.

What does Jesus say will happen to the person who exalts himself?

Is there any room for excuses when salvation is offered?

What must we carry to follow Christ?

Research study questions; refer to scripture cross-references.

Was Jesus invited to this feast to be caught off guard? Was the ploy successful? John 2:24, 25.

Who is the example of true humility? Phil. 2:1–16. What does Solomon say on the subject of seating? Prov. 25:6, 7.

Where does Jesus want Christians to go to with the gospel message? Mark 16:15.

Record your answer to these self-examination questions.

How does my legalism hinder others from coming to Christ?

When I invite others for a meal, what is my motive?

What excuse do I make when Jesus calls?

Respond to God in prayer and praise.

Ask for deliverance from legalism. Pray for grace to take the lowly place. Pray for a readiness to accept the Master's invitation.

Luke

15

Jesus teaches parables of the lost sheep, lost coin, and the prodigal son.

Read prayerfully the following sections.

Ch. 15:1–7	Jesus points out in the parable of the lost sheep that He receives sinners.
Ch. 15:8–10	Jesus pursues the topic of repentance with the story of the lost coin.
Ch. 15:11–32	Jesus persists with His teaching that God seeks sinners with the account of the lost son.

Review the passage and answer these context questions.

To whom does Jesus liken tax collectors and sinners?

Did the father correct the son when he stated that he was not worthy?

What did the father do when the elder son became angry?

Research study questions; refer to scripture cross-references.

David was a shepherd who, on at least two occasions, risked his life for his sheep. What other Old Testament character dedicated his life to caring for his uncle's sheep for twenty years? Gen. 31:38, 39.

The elder brother had a bad attitude toward his younger brother—he did not want him forgiven. What does the Bible teach on this subject? Matt. 18:15–35; Gal. 6:1–5; 1 John 3:11–24.

Record your answer to these self-examination questions.

Where can I trust God to lead me when I realize I have lost my way?

When was the last time I rejoiced over someone finding salvation?

Have I confessed my sin before my heavenly Father? When was I reconciled?

Respond to God in prayer and praise.

Praise God that He seeks sinners. Ask for help to respond to God's prompting. Pray for friends and family members to respond to God's calling.

Luke 16

Jesus speaks of poor, rich men and also of a rich, poor man.

Read prayerfully the following sections.

Ch. 16:1–15	Jesus relates how a rich man's irresponsible manager responded.
Ch. 16:16–18	Jesus reinforces the Law on divorce and adultery.
Ch. 16:19–31	Jesus recalls the story of a rich man's regret and a poor man's rest.

Review the passage and answer these context questions.

What is commendable about the shrewd manager?

What did the Pharisees love more than God?

What is the lesson to be learned from the rich man and Lazarus?

Research study questions; refer to scripture cross-references.

As Christian stewards, what are our responsibilities? 1 Cor. 4:2; 1 Pet. 4:10. Name some things of which we are to be stewards.

In a materialistic world, how often is money the cause of divorce?

In this story, the poor man is named. Could it be a true story rather than a parable? What can be learned from the rich man's prayer in hell (Hades)?

Record your answer to these self-examination questions.

How am I preparing for the future? What is my attitude to wealth?

How seriously do I take the words of Jesus on divorce and adultery?

How often do I shun the poor and destitute because they "offend" me?

Respond to God in prayer and praise.

Ask for a greater desire to change for the better.
Ask for a greater understanding of the sanctity of marriage. Praise God for the hope of heaven.

Luke

17

Jesus teaches on forgiveness, service, and the coming kingdom.

Read prayerfully the following sections.

Ch. 17:1–6	Jesus speaks of forgiving our brother every time.
Ch. 17:7–10	Jesus stresses faithfulness to duty no matter what the demands.
Ch. 17:11–19	Jesus singles out a cleansed, grateful Samaritan as more worthy.
Ch. 17:20–37	With past events, Jesus symbolizes signs of His coming kingdom.

Review the passage and answer these context questions.

In the opening verses of this chapter, what was Jesus teaching?

What is the lesson to be learned from the grateful leper?

Following the logic of the illustrations, who will be taken when Jesus is revealed?

Research study questions; refer to scripture cross-references.

Should we keep a record of others' offenses? 1 Cor. 13:4–6. What does Paul say we should do when someone wrongs us? Gal. 6:1; Eph. 4:32.

What example of servanthood did Jesus set? Luke 22:27; Phil. 2:6–8.

What springs from an ungrateful heart? Rom. 1:21.

Record your answer to these self-examination questions.

How many times am I prepared to forgive a person who offends me?

How often do I expect praise for just doing my job?

When God answers my prayer, how often do I remember to thank Him?

What preparation have I made for Jesus' return?

Respond to God in prayer and praise.

Ask for grace to exercise forgiveness. Ask for greater faithfulness in service. Ask for a greater desire to see prayers answered.

Luke 18

Jesus teaches on prayer and the criteria for entrance to heaven.

Read prayerfully the following sections.

Ch. 18:1–14	Jesus preaches about a widow, a Pharisee, and a tax collector.
Ch. 18:15–17	Jesus reproves the disciples and appeals to children to come to Him.
Ch. 18:18–30	Jesus presents the commandments and the cost of discipleship to a rich ruler.
Ch. 18:31–43	Jesus predicts His death and causes a blind man to praise God.

Review the passage and answer these context questions.

How do we know God will hear when we pray?

What does Jesus say about looking down on others?

Why did the rich ruler find it difficult to follow Jesus?

Research study questions; refer to scripture cross-references.

What does Luke, the doctor, teach regarding widows? Luke 2:37, 38; 4:25, 26; 7:11–17; 20:45–47; 21:2–4.

The twelve disciples did not have the same compassion as Jesus. On what other occasions did they attempt to send people away? Matt. 14:15; 15:21–23.

If the Law cannot save, what was the purpose of the Law? Rom. 3:19, 20; Gal. 3:19–25.

Record your answer to these self-examination questions.

What attitude should I have when I pray?

How childlike is my faith?

What does Jesus expect me to willingly give up to follow Him?

Respond to God in prayer and praise.

Pray for a humble heart. Praise God that children can come to Him. Ask for a deepening desire to follow Jesus. Ask for perseverance in prayer until the answer is known.

Jesus converts Zacchaeus, teaches stewardship, and enters city.

Read prayerfully the following sections.

Ch. 19:1–10	Jesus calls Zacchaeus the tax collector, who experiences a change.
Ch. 19:11–27	Jesus cites parable comparing different types of servants.
Ch. 19:28–44	Jesus rides a donkey to Jerusalem, and the crowd welcomes Him.
Ch. 19:45–48	Jesus cleanses the temple by casting out moneychangers.

Review the passage and answer these context questions.

What type of sinner was Zacchaeus?

When did the people think the kingdom would come?

Who called out Jesus' praise as He approached Jerusalem?

Research study questions; refer to scripture cross-references.

In the conversion of Zacchaeus, who was doing the seeking? Luke 19:3, 10; Rom. 3:11. What does the Old Testament instruct regarding restitution? Lev. 6:1–7.

What is the difference between the parable of the talents and this story? Matt. 25:14–30.

Did the crowd acknowledge Jesus as king because they thought He would remove the Romans? Zech. 9:9–19. What was their attitude later? Matt. 27:20–26.

Record your answer to these self-examination questions.

Why should I seek amends when I hurt others?

What responsibilities has God given me?

When have I shown willingness to obey the Lord's command?

Respond to God in prayer and praise.

Ask for the courage to make restitution when required.
Pray for help to use the gifts God has given us. Give glory to God in the highest!

Luke 20

Jesus is challenged on authority, taxes, resurrection, and His credentials.

Read prayerfully the following sections.

Ch. 20:1–8	Teachers of the Law, elders, and chief priests challenge Jesus.
Ch. 20:9–18	Jesus tells parable of irresponsible tenants who will be held accountable.
Ch. 20:19–26	Teachers try to trick Jesus on the paying of taxes.
Ch. 20:27–47	Sadducees try to trap Jesus on the resurrection, and Jesus warns the disciples.

Review the passage and answer these context questions.

What was Jesus illustrating in the parable of the tenants?

How did Jesus silence His accusers?

In what way did Moses teach the resurrection?

Research study questions; refer to scripture cross-references.

Why did Jesus refuse to answer the Pharisees' questions? Use the following verses to help find the answer. John 1:15–34.

What verse in Ps. 118 did Jesus quote to prove that He was God's appointee?

What do these verses teach on God's institution of political authorities? Dan. 2:21, 37, 38; Rom. 13; 1 Pet. 2:11–17.

Record your answer to these self-examination questions.

How can I follow Jesus' example when challenged on the subject of authority?

How do I treat God's appointees: with honor and respect or subversive belittling?

When have I used flattery to cover my critical motives?

Respond to God in prayer and praise.

Ask for a greater obedience to God's authority. Praise God for Jesus the capstone (cornerstone). Ask for help to fulfill all your responsibilities.

Jesus comments on widow's offering and gives discourse on end times.

Read prayerfully the following sections.

Ch. 21:1–4	Jesus teaches His disciples a lesson on true giving.
Ch. 21:5–28	Jesus testifies of the terrors that will precede the end times.
Ch. 21:29–33	Jesus tells the parable of the fig tree to illustrate His coming.
Ch. 21:34–38	Jesus teaches disciples to watch and be ready for His coming.

Review the passage and answer these context questions.

Why did Jesus commend the widow's offering?

What warnings did Jesus give for events that are still to come?

What should the believer's attitude be in daily life?

Research study questions; refer to scripture cross-references.

The Jewish nation was looking for a sign regarding Christ's coming. What should the church be looking for? Phil. 3:20, 21.

The fig tree in Scripture usually refers to Israel. Hos. 9:10; Luke 13:6–9. Was Jesus referring to all nations when He makes reference to all the trees?

How should we be praying regarding Jesus' Second Coming? Rev. 22:20.

Record your answer to these self-examination questions.

How often have I presented myself to God?

How willing am I to witness for Jesus in time of persecution?

How does my lifestyle show my expectancy of Jesus' return?

Respond to God in prayer and praise.

Ask for a greater generosity of spirit. Ask for discernment so as not to be deceived. Praise God that Jesus is coming soon.

Luke 22:1–53

Jesus is betrayed by Judas and arrested after the Last Supper.

Read prayerfully the following sections.

Ch. 22:1–6	Judas discusses with authorities how he might betray Jesus.
Ch. 22:7–38	Jesus desires to dine with disciples and details the Lord's Supper.
Ch. 22:39–46	Jesus draws apart at Gethsemane and prays for deliverance.
Ch. 22:47–53	Judas betrays Jesus by delivering Him to the temple soldiers.

Review the passage and answer these context questions.

What motivated Judas to betray Jesus?

What did Jesus ask the disciples to pray?

What request had Satan made of Jesus?

Research study questions; refer to scripture cross-references.

Was Judas ever a true believer? Had he ever received the cleansing that Jesus brought? John 6:64–70; 13:10, 11.

Peter tried to fight the wrong enemy with the wrong weapon. What enemy should he have been fighting, and what weapons should he have been using? 2 Cor. 10:3–6; Eph. 6:10–18.

Why did the chief priests and temple guard choose such an isolated place to arrest Jesus? Matt. 26:4, 5; Mark 14:1, 2; Luke 19:47.

Record your answer to these self-examination questions.

What value do I put on money? How often does it come between Jesus and me?

How often do I want the best for myself at the expense of others?

How does Jesus expect me to treat those who have hurt me?

Respond to God in prayer and praise.

Ask for grace to never fall away. Ask for a desire to meet with God's people.
Praise God that Jesus came to do the Father's will.

Luke 22:54—23:25

Jesus is disowned, mocked, and tried before chief priests, Pilate, and Herod.

Read prayerfully the following sections.

Ch. 22:54–62	Peter denies Jesus then remembers Jesus' words.
Ch. 22:63–71	Jesus is mocked and beaten by soldiers then questioned by the chief priests.
Ch. 23:1–6	Jesus is charged before Pilate and declared innocent but sent to Herod.
Ch. 23:7–25	Jesus is questioned, accused, ridiculed, and then found guilty by Pilate.

Review the passage and answer these context questions.

Who did Jesus claim to be?

Why did Pilate send Jesus to be tried by Herod?

On what ground did Pilate hand Jesus over to be crucified?

Research study questions; refer to scripture cross-references.

Was Peter supposed to be following Jesus at this time? Matt. 26:31; John 18:8, 9. What made Peter an easy target for Satan's temptation? Matt. 26:33–35.

According to Peter's epistles, how should we react when sinners mock and ridicule us because of our faith? 1 Pet. 2:18–25.

Pilate went down in history as a pathetic case of indecisiveness. Is there any excuse for this lack of character? Matt. 27:24, 25; Mark 15:15; John 18:29–38; 19:1–13.

Record your answer to these self-examination questions.

How do I know that Jesus is the Son of God?

How does my Christianity stand up in the secular world?

What should I do when people falsely accuse me? Whose example should I follow?

Respond to God in prayer and praise.

Ask for courage always to testify association with Jesus.
Pray for a better understanding of the great cost of salvation. Praise God that Jesus was sinless.

Luke 23:26–56

Jesus is crucified, dies, and His body is placed in a tomb.

Read prayerfully the following sections.

Ch. 23:26–43	Jesus is crucified between criminals and calls for pardon for scoffers.
Ch. 23:44–49	Jesus commits His spirit to God and dies; a centurion believes.
Ch. 23:50–56	Joseph clothes Christ's body in linen cloth, placing it in a tomb.

Review the passage and answer these context questions.

Did Simon voluntarily carry Jesus' cross?

What did the religious leaders say and do when Jesus hung on the cross?

How many hours of darkness shrouded the scene?

Research study questions; refer to scripture cross-references.

How can one know the meaning and purpose of Jesus' death? Is. 53:10–12?

Jesus did not make an offering for His own sins. Whose sins did He die for?

Who was Joseph, and who accompanied him in his mission? John 19:38–42.

How was Isaiah 53:9 fulfilled?

Record your answer to these self-examination questions.

How willing am I to take up my cross and follow Jesus?

How fickle am I in following the majority?

In what way am I watching and waiting to care for the needs of others?

Respond to God in prayer and praise.

Praise God for the pardon Jesus brings. Ask for spiritual eyes to see Jesus. Pray for a more compassionate heart.

Jesus is raised, seen by many, commissions disciples, and ascends to heaven.

Read prayerfully the following sections.

Ch. 24:1–12	Angels announce Jesus' resurrection to alarmed women.
Ch. 24:13–35	Jesus appears to two on the Emmaus road.
Ch. 24:36–49	Jesus appears and stands among the disciples.
Ch. 24:50–53	Jesus ascends to heaven as the disciples worship.

Review the passage and answer these context questions.

Who was the first to declare that Jesus was risen from the dead?

What had Jesus stated regarding His resurrection?

Why did the two on the Emmaus road not recognize Jesus?

Research study questions; refer to scripture cross-references.

When had Jesus told the disciples that these events concerning His death and resurrection would take place? Luke 9:22; 18:33. Why did the women and the disciples not remember? Luke 24:25.

Is the word "eleven," when referring to the disciples, used only in a collective sense? Mark 16:14; John 20:24.

The resurrection body of Christ was the same body that was buried, with some differences. What were some of these? Luke 24:51; John 20:19.

Record your answer to these self-examination questions.

How can I have courage when proclaiming what seems nonsensical to the world?

If asked, how could I prove who Jesus was?

When did I come to believe that Jesus is truly risen from the dead?

Respond to God in prayer and praise.

Praise God that Jesus is risen from the dead. Pray for a greater understanding of prophecy. Ask for a greater obedience to the Great Commission.

John 1:1–18

God the Son becomes man to make us God's children.

Read prayerfully the following sections.

Ch. 1:1–5	John declares the eternal Son, creator of all things, bringing life and light.
Ch. 1:6–9	John the Baptist proclaims that Jesus would be the true Light.
Ch. 1:10–18	John states that those who recognize Jesus receive grace and blessing.

Review the passage and answer these context questions.

Who was with God the Father in the beginning?

What does Jesus give to those who believe in Him?

Who did Jesus make known when He became flesh?

Research study questions; refer to scripture cross-references.

What does Jesus say in relation to Abraham that leaves no doubt He always existed? John 8:57, 58.

How did Jesus rank John the Baptist as a witness? Matt. 11:7–11. How many miracles did John perform? John 10:41.

Why was it important that Jesus was not born of natural descent? Rom. 5:12–17; 1 Cor. 15:22; Heb. 4:15.

Record your answer to these self-examination questions.

How much of my life is under God's control?

Does my witness of Jesus to others proclaim Him or me?

What blessings have I received through Jesus Christ?

Respond to God in prayer and praise.

Praise God the Father for His eternal Son. Praise God for Jesus the Light of the world. Praise God for the blessings that are in Jesus.

John 1:19–51

John the Baptist and the first disciples testify who Jesus is.

Read prayerfully the following sections.

Ch. 1:19–28	John the Baptist denies he is Elijah or the Messiah.
Ch. 1:29–34	John testifies that the Holy Spirit has verified who Jesus is.
Ch. 1:35–42	John's disciples follow Jesus and then witness to others.
Ch. 1:43–51	Philip and Nathanael believe who Jesus is and follow Him.

Review the passage and answer these context questions.

What did John the Baptist testify concerning the pre-existence of Jesus?

Whom did Andrew say he had found?

Why did Nathanael testify that Jesus was deity?

Research study questions; refer to scripture cross-references.

What can we read of "the Prophet" that the priests and the Levites asked John about? Deut. 18:15, 18.

Other references in the New Testament speak of Jesus as the Lamb. What can be learned from them? 1 Pet. 1:18, 19; Rev. 5:6; 7:14.

Who else saw angels ascending and descending? Does it mean that heaven is now open as a result of Christ's death and resurrection? Gen. 28:12.

Record your answer to these self-examination questions.

What is my attitude, compared to John's, when testifying of Christ to others?

Have I acknowledged Jesus as the Lamb who took away my sin?

How am I following Jesus and bringing others to know Him?

Respond to God in prayer and praise.

Praise God that Jesus is the Messiah. Ask for a heart to respond when God speaks. Ask for help to follow Jesus.

John 2

Jesus changes water into wine and cleanses the temple.

Read prayerfully the following sections.

Ch. 2:1–11	Jesus performs His first miracle at Cana by turning water to wine.
Ch. 2:12–22	Jesus purifies the polluted temple and is challenged by the Jews.
Ch. 2:23–25	Jesus presents Himself at the Passover, but is careful of popularity.

Review the passage and answer these context questions.

What was the twofold purpose of this miracle?

For what purpose did Jesus use the whip of cords?

Did the disciples know what Jesus meant when He rebuked the Jews?

Research study questions; refer to scripture cross-references.

Whose wedding might Jesus have been attending due to the fact that Mary and His brothers were present also? John 2:12; Matt. 13:55, 56.

The disciples saw Jesus' zeal in cleansing the temple and remembered the Psalm that spoke of this. How many other things can be listed from this one Psalm that speak of Christ? Ps. 69.

Where in John's Gospel does Jesus promise He will entrust Himself to those who truly believe?

Record your answer to these self-examination questions.

What is my reaction when I am asked to do something to help others?

From what sins do I need to be cleansed?

How do outward manifestations of so-called miracles sway my belief? What is required?

Respond to God in prayer and praise.

Ask for help to do what Jesus commands. Ask for daily cleansing from sin. Praise God that Jesus is all-knowing.

Nicodemus interviews Jesus; John declares Jesus the Messiah.

Read prayerfully the following sections.

Ch. 3:1–15	Jesus debates with Nicodemus about the new birth.
Ch. 3:16–21	Jesus delivers the gospel in the clearest of forms.
Ch. 3:22–36	John declares Jesus the Messiah when questioned by his disciples.

Review the passage and answer these context questions.

Nicodemus knew that Jesus came from God. Was that enough?

Why do evil men not come into the Light?

If one does not accept Jesus' testimony, what does that imply?

Research study questions; refer to scripture cross-references.

Was Nicodemus, the ruling Pharisee, ever born again? John 7:50; 19:38–42.

Was there anyone for whom Jesus did not die? John 3:16.

Had John, or have we, any right of complaint as to the position or mission God has called us to? 1 Cor. 12:12–31.

Record your answer to these self-examination questions.

In what ways am I faithfully proclaiming the necessity of being born again?

How do my deeds bear up to the scrutiny of Jesus, the Way, the Truth and the Light?

How do I express joy when God's Word is spoken?

Respond to God in prayer and praise.

Ask for a clearer understanding of the new birth. Praise God for the simplicity of the gospel. Ask for more opportunities to testify that Jesus is the Messiah.

John 4:1–42

Jesus talks with a Samaritan woman and her townspeople believe.

Read prayerfully the following sections.

Ch. 4:1–15	Jesus offers a surprised Samaritan woman living water.
Ch. 4:16–26	Surprised by Jesus' knowledge of her, she desires to know more.
Ch. 4:27–38	Surprised disciples rejoin Jesus as He speaks of their mission.
Ch. 4:39–42	Hometown accepts woman's testimony and believes.

Review the passage and answer these context questions.

How did Jesus break the mold of Jewish practices?

How does Jesus say we should worship God?

Whom did the Samaritans recognize Him to be?

Research study questions; refer to scripture cross-references.

Jesus broke the silence of racial prejudice and spoke first. Who spoke first when Adam sinned? Gen. 3:9. How did God first show His love for us? John 3:16; Rom. 5:8.

How did Jesus know that this woman had had five husbands? John 1:48.

What was God's plan and will for Jesus?

Record your answer to these self-examination questions.

In what way have I shared the good news with other ethnic groups?

What has been my reaction when the Holy Spirit has revealed my past?

How has sharing the gospel become my meat and drink?

Respond to God in prayer and praise.

Praise God for the Fountain of Living Water. Ask for a deepening desire to know more about God. Ask for a greater burden to share the message with others.

John 4:43—5:47

Jesus heals a child and a paralytic, and then testimonials are given.

Read prayerfully the following sections.

Ch. 4:43–54	Jesus heeds the request from an official regarding his child.
Ch. 5:1–15	Jesus heals a paralytic on the Sabbath at the pool of Bethesda.
Ch. 5:16–30	Jesus has equality with God, so He has power to judge and give life.
Ch. 5:31–47	Jesus is held to be God's Son by four testimonials.

Review the passage and answer these context questions.

What convinced the royal official to believe in Jesus?

What can be learned from the Jews' reaction when they first spotted the lame walking?

What testimonies are there of Jesus' credentials?

Research study questions; refer to scripture cross-references.

Name the prophet who Jesus uses as an illustration to prove what is said in chapter 4 verse 44? Luke 4:24, 25.

What does the book of Nehemiah say about the "sheep gate"? Neh. 3:1; 12:39.

John states that there are only two classes of people. Who are they? 1 John 5:12.

Record your answer to these self-examination questions.

How do I show that I believe in the power of Jesus?

How do I respond when Jesus asks of me what appears to be the impossible?

When did I cross over from death into life? How are my actions pleasing to God?

Respond to God in prayer and praise.

Ask for more faith to take Jesus at His word.
Ask for more compassion for the helpless. Praise God that Jesus is the only judge.

John 6:1–21

By feeding five thousand and walking on water, Jesus tests disciples' faith.

Read prayerfully the following sections.

Ch. 6:1–13	Jesus works a miracle by feeding five thousand.
Ch. 6:14–15	Jesus withdraws from the multitude, desiring not to be part of a mob.
Ch. 6:16–21	Jesus walks on water and calms the frightened disciples.

Review the passage and answer these context questions.

Why did the crowds follow Jesus?

How did Jesus react when they wanted to make Him king?

Did the disciples recognize Jesus when they saw Him walking on the water?

Research study questions; refer to scripture cross-references.

How many people did Jesus literally feed with the five loaves and two fish? Matt. 14:21.

What did the multitude need to recognize in Jesus before they could make Him king? Acts 4:12.

The disciples in the storm thought Jesus had deserted them. Will Jesus ever leave us to face the difficulties of life alone? Heb. 13:5. According to Matthew's Gospel, what did Peter attempt to do? Matt. 14:28–32.

Record your answer to these self-examination questions.

How can I use my gifts to help those in need?

How am I tempted to put my personal ambitions before God's plan?

In what way can I experience Jesus in the midst of life's storms?

Respond to God in prayer and praise.

Pray for victory when tested. Ask for patience to wait for heaven's kingdom. Praise God for the peace Jesus brings.

John 6:22–71

Jesus delivers four messages about the Bread that gives life.

Read prayerfully the following sections.

Ch. 6:22–40	Jesus claims He is the Bread of Life to the miracle-seeking crowd.
Ch. 6:41–51	Jesus cites scripture as grumbling Jews discuss His origin.
Ch. 6:52–59	Jesus tells arguing Jews that man must feed on Him.
Ch. 6:60–71	Jesus challenges His disciples as some turn from following Him.

Review the passage and answer these context questions.

On whom did God place His seal of approval?

How does Jesus say we receive the Bread of Life?

What will happen to the person who believes in Jesus?

Research study questions; refer to scripture cross-references.

Like the seeking crowd, the jailer at Philippi wanted to do something to be saved. What was Paul's answer, and how did they respond? Acts 16:31–33.

How does God the Father draw people to trust in Christ? Can the believer be used by God to draw people? John 16:8–11; 2 Cor. 3:3, 5.

Does the statement, "eats my flesh and drinks my blood," refer to the communion service, or does it refer to appropriating by faith the work of Christ on the cross? 1 John 1:7.

Record your answer to these self-examination questions.

How do I show that my desires are not for wealth but for enduring realities?

In what ways am I teaching others to listen to the Word of God?

When did I come to realize that those who feed on Christ will live forever?

Respond to God in prayer and praise.

Praise God that Jesus is the Bread of Life.
Ask for words to draw others to Jesus. Pray for a daily desire to feed on Him.

John 7

Jesus attends the Feast of Tabernacles and teaches a divided audience.

Read prayerfully the following sections.

Ch. 7:1–13	Jesus decides it's the right time to attend the Feast of Tabernacles.
Ch. 7:14–36	Pharisaical duplicity is revealed when Jesus teaches He is of God.
Ch. 7:37–44	Crowd is divided as Jesus promises believers the Holy Spirit.
Ch. 7:45–53	Nicodemus demands fair hearing for Jesus, but Pharisees refuse.

Review the passage and answer these context questions.

What were the crowds saying about Jesus?

On the subject of the Sabbath, how were the Jews contradicting themselves?

Why did the temple guard not arrest Jesus?

Research study questions; refer to scripture cross-references.

The ancient Jewish historian, Josephus, calls the Feast of Tabernacles the most holy of all the Hebrew feasts. What details can be discovered about this feast? Lev. 23:33–44.

One of the rituals associated with the feast was that each day the priest went to the pool of Siloam with a golden drinking cup and later with great pomp and ceremony poured the water on the altar in the temple. Jesus used the occasion to speak of the outpouring of the Holy Spirit. When did this outpouring take place? Acts 2:1–13.

Record your answer to these self-examination questions.

How often do I take my guidance from others? Where can I find guidance?

In what way do I allow legalism to stop me from being effective in service?

When speaking about spiritual things do I give others a fair hearing?

Respond to God in prayer and praise.

Pray for a greater willingness to seek divine guidance.
Praise God for the deity of Christ. Ask for more patience to listen when others speak.

John 8:1–11

Pharisees bring a woman caught in adultery to Jesus, hoping to trap Him.

Read prayerfully the following sections.

Ch. 8:1–2	Jesus chooses solitude then returns to teach at dawn.
Ch. 8:3–6	Pharisees charge an adulterous woman, trying to trap Jesus in a point of law.
Ch. 8:7–9	Jesus challenges the Pharisees to stone her if they are without sin.
Ch. 8:10–11	Jesus challenges the woman to leave her life of sin.

Review the passage and answer these context questions.

What act revealed that the Pharisees had no compassion for the woman?

What was Jesus' answer to their many questions?

What did Jesus ask the sinful woman to do?

Research study questions; refer to scripture cross-references.

Does this disputed passage, which does not appear in some manuscripts, fit the context?

What was the punishment for a woman caught in the act of adultery? Deut. 22:22.

Whose finger wrote the Ten Commandments at Mt. Sinai? Could He have written the same thing here? Deut. 9:10.

Does repentance and confession only mean being sorry for one's sin? What else is involved? Luke 11:24–28.

Record your answer to these self-examination questions.

How much time do I spend alone in God's presence?

How does pride prevent me from seeing my own sin?

How does God's Word make me aware of sin?

Respond to God in prayer and praise.

Pray for a greater desire to spend time alone with God.
Ask for grace, not condemnation, for others. Praise God for His great mercy.

John 8:12–59

Jesus teaches light, truth, and freedom to all who believe.

Read prayerfully the following sections.

Ch. 8:12–20 Jesus' validity as the Light of the world comes from the Father.
Ch. 8:21–30 Jesus voices challenge to vacillating Jews to believe or die in their sin.
Ch. 8:31–59 Jesus verifies His divine credentials, claiming His truth brings freedom.

Review the passage and answer these context questions.

Did Jesus deny that He testified of Himself?

What is the devil's native language? John 8:44.

Who does Jesus say existed before Abraham?

Research study questions; refer to scripture cross-references.

At the time Jesus said, "I am the Light of the world," the priest would have been proclaiming that the Messiah would be a light to the Gentiles. What did Isaiah say about this? Is. 42:6, 7.

What did Jesus mean about the Son of man being lifted up? John 3:14; John 12:32.

What were the "things, which Abraham did," that Jesus alluded to? Rom. 4:1–5. To what type of death in verse 51 was Jesus referring? Rev. 20:12–15.

Record your answer to these self-examination questions.

How much light does my faith give to those walking in the darkness of unbelief?

What challenges am I giving to unbelievers?

What sinful habits or faithless attitudes do I need to be set free from?

Respond to God in prayer and praise.

Praise God for Jesus, the Light of the world. Ask for faith to believe the gospel message. Pray for freedom from the bondage of sin.

John 9

Jesus heals a blind man on the Sabbath and the Pharisees investigate.

Read prayerfully the following sections.

Ch. 9:1–12	Jesus displays God's power by healing a blind man.
Ch. 9:13–34	Pharisees demand answers from blind man and his parents to verify healing.
Ch. 9:35–41	Jesus discloses His identity to the blind man, who finds faith.

Review the passage and answer these context questions.

Why was this particular man born blind?

What did this man appear to receive as well as his sight?

What happens to those who think they see but refuse Jesus?

Research study questions; refer to scripture cross-references.

Which of the commandments were the disciples alluding to when they suggested that the man was suffering because of his parents' sin? Ex. 20:4, 6.

Why, in most of Jesus' miracles, does Jesus ask for some action before healing takes place? Which miracle by Elisha also required washing? 2 Kgs. 5:1–14.

Were the Pharisees, by calling out to the man's parents in the crowd, trying to intimidate them? Did it work?

Record your answer to these self-examination questions.

How willing am I to obey God's commands so that my life can be changed?

In what way is my faith being strengthened on a daily basis?

When did I discover that without Christ I was spiritually blind?

Respond to God in prayer and praise.

Ask for a willingness to accept God's guidance.
Pray for an understanding of the will of God. Praise God for the light of the gospel.

John 10

Jesus, the Good Shepherd, gives care and security to His sheep.

Read prayerfully the following sections.

Ch. 10:1–21	Jesus teaches the parable of the good shepherd.
Ch. 10:22–30	Jesus tells unbelieving Jews His sheep have security in Him.
Ch. 10:31–42	Jews throw charges of blasphemy at Jesus' claim to deity.

Review the passage and answer these context questions.

Was there any other way for the sheep to enter the sheepfold?

What made the Jews think Jesus was mad?

What actions of Jesus should have caused the Jews to believe?

Research study questions; refer to scripture cross-references.

Was Jesus telling the Pharisees they were false shepherds? Where does the Bible speak of such shepherds? Was Jesus afraid of them? Jer. 25:34; Zech. 10:3.

When Jesus states that no one can snatch the believer out of God's hand, does that includes angels and devils? John 3:16, 36.

What scripture was Jesus referring to in verse 34? Ps. 82:6. Was Jesus essentially saying, "even if I were not the Son of God, you still have no right to stone Me"?

Record your answer to these self-examination questions.

When Jesus calls me to follow, how do I respond?

Where do I find the assurance that I am secure in Christ?

How does knowing that Jesus is God affect the way I live?

Respond to God in prayer and praise.

Praise God that Jesus is the Good Shepherd. Pray for the assurance of salvation. Pray for a more receptive heart to the Word of God.

John 11

Jesus raises Lazarus, and the Sanhedrin fear the consequences.

Read prayerfully the following sections.

Ch. 11:1–16	Jesus delays going to Bethany to heal Lazarus.
Ch. 11:17–37	Jesus discourses with sisters and comforts them.
Ch. 11:38–44	Jesus delivers Lazarus from among the dead.
Ch. 11:45–57	Pharisees deviously plot to arrest and kill Jesus.

Review the passage and answer these context questions.

Why did Jesus not heed the sisters' call immediately?

Why did Jesus weep?

What caused Caiaphas to suggest Jesus' death?

Research study questions; refer to scripture cross-references.

Why was Jesus not afraid to return to the place of danger when all His disciples were? John 7:6; Matt. 26:45. Can you understand why by the answer He gives?

What did Jesus mean when He said, "whoever lives and believes in me will never die"? 1 Cor. 15:12–22.

What is the difference between true resurrection and Lazarus' resurrection? John 3:36; 1 Cor. 15; Rev. 2:11; 20:11–15.

Record your answer to these self-examination questions.

How is my faith strengthened when God allows my circumstances to grow worse?

What impossible situation am I trusting God to change?

When was I freed from the grave clothes of sin?

How can I help to change people's preconceived ideas about Jesus?

Respond to God in prayer and praise.

Ask for more patience to wait for God's timing.
Praise God for the compassion of Jesus. Praise God for the deliverance He brings.

John 12:1–19

Mary anoints Jesus, who then triumphantly enters Jerusalem.

Read prayerfully the following sections.

Ch. 12:1–3	Mary selflessly sacrifices expensive perfume to anoint Jesus.
Ch. 12:4–11	Judas shamefully objects to Mary's action, but Jesus defends her.
Ch. 12:12–19	Crowd spectacularly welcomes Jesus as He enters city.

Review the passage and answer these context questions.

What motivated Judas to object?

Who else was on the chief priest's death list?

Who did the people think Jesus was at this point?

Research study questions; refer to scripture cross-references.

Matthew, who presents Jesus as King, states that Mary anointed His head. Mark, who presents Jesus as servant, states she broke the jar. Luke and John emphasise that it was His feet she anointed. What was the real impact of her actions? Matt. 26:7; Mark 14:3; Luke 7:38.

Was the crowd fickle in their praise? Mark 15:11–15. Which verse in Psalm 118 gives the detail of this event and speaks also of Jesus coming at the Second Advent?

Record your answer to these self-examination questions.

What is my attitude toward giving, and what can I give that is precious to me?

How do I rate as a steward? How often do I cheat and then sit in judgment on others?

In what way does my voice praise and magnify the King of Kings?

Respond to God in prayer and praise.

Pray for a deeper appreciation of the person of Christ.
Praise God that Jesus receives our gifts. Ask for direction in how to worship.

John 12:20–50

Jesus predicts His death, heaven is moved, and many refuse Him.

Read prayerfully the following sections.

Ch. 12:20–22	Greek proselytes ask to meet with Jesus.
Ch. 12:23–36	Jesus predicts His death, prays, and the crowd hears heaven respond.
Ch. 12:37–50	Jews protest Jesus' claim, but Jesus reiterates salvation plan.

Review the passage and answer these context questions.

What did Jesus have to say about the Greeks?

What was the purpose of the voice?

What did Isaiah see when he wrote about Jesus?

Research study questions; refer to scripture cross-references.

Why did the disciples discuss the Greeks' request to see Jesus? Matt. 10:5, 6.

When Jesus states, "unless a kernel of wheat falls to the ground and dies, it remains only a single seed," does He mean that apart from the cross there can be no spiritual harvest? Matt. 10:37–39; 16:26; Luke 17:32, 33.

What did Jesus mean when He said, "a man who hates his life will keep it"? How does Paul link confession with salvation? Rom. 4:1–8; 10:9; Eph. 2:8, 9.

Record your answer to these self-examination questions.

When I come to worship, who is my focus?

In what way am I following Jesus' example as I seek to serve others?

How does my fear of losing popularity keep me from openly acknowledging Jesus?

Respond to God in prayer and praise.

Pray for a greater desire to learn more about Jesus. Praise God that Jesus is glorified. Ask for simplicity of words to share the gospel with others.

John 13

Jesus washes the disciples' feet and announces His betrayal and Peter's denial.

Read prayerfully the following sections.

Ch. 13:1–11	Jesus takes a towel and washes His disciples' feet.
Ch. 13:12–17	Jesus teaches disciples to serve others humbly.
Ch. 13:18–30	Jesus, troubled in spirit, predicts Judas will betray Him.
Ch. 13:31–38	Jesus tells disciples of His departure and predicts Peter's denial.

Review the passage and answer these context questions.

How did Jesus show His disciples the full extent of His love?

How did Jesus feel when He thought of Judas?

How are Jesus' disciples identified?

Research study questions; refer to scripture cross-references.

Was it because no one else was willing to do this task that Jesus took the lowest place and washed His disciples' feet? Luke 22:24.

What do Paul's letters say about Jesus' example of humility, and what can be learned from this attitude? Phil. 2:5–11.

Where was Jesus going that Peter could not follow, but would follow later? John 21:18, 19.

Record your answer to these self-examination questions.

How am I cleansed and made fit for service?

What can I do to be protected from the evil that Satan plans for me?

In what ways have I disowned Jesus in the company of others?

Respond to God in prayer and praise.

Pray for cleansing from sin and failure. Pray for more humility to serve others.
Praise God that Jesus knows and cares.

John 14:1–14

Jesus, the Way, the Truth, and the Life, promises to return.

Read prayerfully the following sections.

Ch. 14:1–4	Jesus comforts disciples, promising He will return.
Ch. 14:5–7	Jesus conveys to Thomas that He is the Way, the Truth, and the Life.
Ch. 14:8–14	Jesus clarifies to Philip that He and the Father are one.

Review the passage and answer these context questions.

What is the answer to a troubled heart?

How do we see God the Father?

In whose name do we make our requests?

Research study questions; refer to scripture cross-references.

In what way has Jesus made preparation for us-past, present, and future? Rom. 5:9; 6:5; 1 Pet. 1:4.

When will all our doubts and unbelief, like Thomas', disappear? John 20:24–28; 1 John 3:1, 2.

Did Philip have any excuse for demanding to see the Father? As Jesus rebuked him, what proofs did Jesus give that He and the Father were one?

Record your answer to these self-examination questions.

When life gets me down, what do I have to look forward to?

Which or whose way am I following, and will it lead me to God?

How can I pray with confidence that God will answer?

Respond to God in prayer and praise.

Praise God that Jesus is returning. Pray for clear direction and certainty in decision-making. Praise God for the uniqueness of Jesus.

John 14:15–31

Jesus promises the Holy Spirit and His comforting peace.

Read prayerfully the following sections.

Ch. 14:15–26	Jesus promises the Holy Spirit's presence to those who love and obey.
Ch. 14:27–31	Jesus promises heavenly peace to combat Satan's worldly influences.

Review the passage and answer these context questions.

How do we show our love for Christ?

Why does Jesus not show Himself to the world today?

What is the difference between the peace of God and the peace of the world?

Research study questions; refer to scripture cross-references.

The Holy Spirit is called "another Counselor," which means another of the same kind. What other names describe His work? Is. 11:2; Zech. 12:10; Mark 1:10; Acts 2:3; Eph. 1:13, 17; 2 Tim. 1:7.

The world can only give temporary peace, but Paul states that God's peace transcends all understanding. What sort of peace does Isaiah the prophet call it? Is. 26:3, 4. Where is Jesus called the Prince of Peace?

Record your answer to these self-examination questions.

Where do I receive teaching that will help me understand the things Jesus taught?

How does my striving and struggling keep me from resting in God's peace?

What can I do when worldly influences threaten to overpower me?

Respond to God in prayer and praise.

Ask for the filling of the Holy Spirit. Praise God for the Holy Spirit. Praise God for the peace Jesus brings.

John 15:1–17

Jesus is the Vine, and believers are fruit-bearing branches.

Read prayerfully the following sections.

Ch. 15:1–5	Abiding branches of the True Vine bear fruit.
Ch. 15:6–8	Alienated branches bear no fruit and are destroyed.
Ch. 15:9–17	Appointed and chosen ones are called to love each other.

Review the passage and answer these context questions.

What fruit can we bear apart from Christ?

What is Jesus' command to His disciples in this chapter?

Who are the friends of Christ?

Research study questions; refer to scripture cross-references.

Who was the unclean one not abiding in the Vine? What previous statement of Jesus discloses this? John 13:10, 11.

There are different branches mentioned: the carnal branch, the spiritual branch, and the unbelieving branch. What does Jesus say will happen to each type? John 15:2, 6.

Is God's love for us independent of our love for Him? John 3:16. What did God do for us while we were still His enemies? Should our love for others be independent of how they feel about us? Rom. 5:8.

Record your answer to these self-examination questions.

How do I accept God's pruning and become more fruitful because of it?

What effort do I make to remain in fellowship so as not to be temporarily cut off?

In what way am I showing God's love to others?

Respond to God in prayer and praise.

Pray for a dedication to Christ that bears fruit. Pray for a desire to see others blessed. Praise God that we are chosen to serve Him.

John 15:18—16:4

Jesus warns of the world's hostility but promises power to overcome.

Read prayerfully the following sections.

Ch. 15:18–21	The world hates and persecutes those who belong to Jesus.
Ch. 15:22–25	The world has heard the message and therefore stands guilty before God.
Ch. 15:26—16:4	The deluded world, by hating believers, thinks it is serving God.

Review the passage and answer these context questions.

What could it mean if the world loves us?

How did the world react to Jesus' miracles?

Why is Jesus warning His disciples at this time?

Research study questions; refer to scripture cross-references.

This passage gives seven reasons why believers are hated by the world. What can we learn from them? John 15:18–25.

The Pharisees and scribes who represent religion hate Jesus' teaching. Should we expect organized religion to like the same message today? Matt. 23:27.

What did Jesus warn His disciples would happen after His arrest? Matt. 26:56.

Record your answer to these self-examination questions.

How does the knowledge that the world hated Jesus help when I am personally rejected?

What have I done with the message of Jesus and how do I stand before God?

In what way do I show my willingness to testify in the face of opposition?

Respond to God in prayer and praise.

Ask for steadfastness when faced with persecution.
Pray for faith to respond to the gospel. Praise God for the martyr's crown.

John 16:5–33

Jesus promises the Holy Spirit will bring conviction, guidance, and joy.

Read prayerfully the following sections.

Ch. 16:5–15	Jesus promises the Holy Spirit's guidance in understanding.
Ch. 16:16–22	Jesus promises complete joy after grief of separation.
Ch. 16:23–33	Jesus promises disciples answered prayer and peace.

Review the passage and answer these context questions.

Where does Satan stand before God today?

What would be the disciples' reaction at the death of Christ?

Why is Jesus warning His disciples about future events?

Research study questions; refer to scripture cross-references.

Why was it advantageous for the physical Jesus to leave the disciples? John 16:7.

What did the Holy Spirit do that enabled the disciples to reveal the things of Christ to us? John 4:24; 14:26; Rom. 8:14, 16; 1 Cor. 12:8–11; 2 Cor. 3:18; Phil. 3:3; 2 Tim. 3:16; 2 Pet. 1:21; 3:15.

What does the Holy Spirit do for the believer after his/her conversion? Acts 1:8.

Record your answer to these self-examination questions.

What joy can I claim when my saved loved ones are taken from me?

How does Jesus give me confidence to pray for my needs?

In what way does Jesus help me overcome the stress and troubles of life?

Respond to God in prayer and praise.

Ask for a greater understanding of God's promises. Praise God for the peace and joy He gives. Ask for more faith to cast your burdens on the Lord.

John 17

Jesus prays for Himself, His disciples, and all believers.

Read prayerfully the following sections.

Ch. 17:1–5	Jesus prays that He will be glorified in heaven.
Ch. 17:6–19	Jesus prays for protection and sanctification for His disciples.
Ch. 17:20–26	Jesus prays for all who will hear and believe the gospel.

Review the passage and answer these context questions.

What is Jesus' definition of eternal life?

What type of protection does Jesus request for His disciples?

Where does Jesus want us to be eventually?

Research study questions; refer to scripture cross-references.

John 17, to be truthful, is really the Lord's Prayer. What scripture is usually called the Lord's Prayer? What should it be called? Matt. 6:9–13.

What difference is there between the one who left heaven and the one who will soon return? Phil. 2:6–11; 1 Cor. 15:42.

What are some differences between those who are of this world and those who are not of this world? John 3:5–8; 8:44; 1 Cor. 6:19, 20.

How many denominations does Jesus desire for believers according to John 17?

Record your answer to these self-examination questions.

What can I do to be more effective in bringing others to know God?

In what ways do I feel protected from the temptations and dangers of our world?

How am I showing God's love to believers? Would my attitude unite or divide?

Respond to God in prayer and praise.

Praise God for Jesus our Great Advocate. Ask for an understanding of how God sees sin. Ask for help to appropriate God's love.

John 18:1–27

Jesus is betrayed, arrested, and questioned while Peter denies Him.

Read prayerfully the following sections.

Ch. 18:1–11	Jesus consents to the Father's will and is arrested.
Ch. 18:12–24	Jesus constrained by soldiers while Peter denies Him.
Ch. 18:25–27	Peter continues to deny Jesus, and a rooster crows—just as Christ predicted.

Review the passage and answer these context questions.

How had Jesus prepared for the event that lay ahead?

Why did Jesus want no resistance to His arrest?

How did Peter compare to Jesus when challenged?

Research study questions; refer to scripture cross-references.

What words caused the arresting soldiers to fall backward when Jesus spoke? Ex. 3:14.

What words of Jesus were fulfilled when He requested the release of His disciples? John 6:39; 17:12. John is the only Gospel that mentions it was Peter who drew his sword. Why might John be the only writer able to name Peter?

Was the official ordered to strike Jesus? Was this a fair trial, or was it rigged to produce a desired result (the death of Jesus)? Luke 22:63–65.

Record your answer to these self-examination questions.

How willing am I to accept the cup of suffering if God gives it to me?

When faced with skeptical questions how can I testify truthfully for Jesus?

How often do my words and actions deny that I belong to Jesus?

Respond to God in prayer and praise.

Praise God that Jesus came to do the Father's will.
Ask for courage in declaring your faith. Ask for forgiveness for those who fail.

John 18:28—19:16

Jesus is questioned, flogged, mocked, and delivered for crucifixion by Pilate.

Read prayerfully the following sections.

Ch. 18:28–40	Pilate interrogates Jesus. Pilate then unsuccessfully seeks to release Him.
Ch. 19:1–5	Jesus is flogged, crowned with thorns, mocked, and physically abused.
Ch. 19:6–16	Pilate seeks a reprieve, but, cowering to pressure, hands Jesus over to be crucified.

Review the passage and answer these context questions.

Did Jesus indicate that He desired to be king over the Jews?

How many times was Jesus struck on the face?

Who was in charge of the situation: Pilate or God?

Research study questions; refer to scripture cross-references.

It was Passover time, and the Jews did not enter the Roman palace for fear of defiling themselves. Did they think that ceremonial defilement was more serious than moral defilement? What did Jesus say about this? Matt. 23:27; Luke 11:39.

What can be learned about Pilate's character from the other Gospels? Matt. 27:19.

What sort of death did Jesus have to die to fulfill scripture? Deut. 21:23; John 3:14; 12:32; Gal. 3:13.

Record your answer to these self-examination questions.

When my beliefs are questioned, how truthful am I?

What helps me when I suffer abuse for being a Christian?

When faced with divided loyalties, does my decision reflect truth or the status quo?

Respond to God in prayer and praise.

Ask for help to testify of Jesus. Praise God for the help of the Holy Spirit. Ask for courage in witnessing.

John 19:17–42

Jesus is crucified between two thieves, dies, and is buried.

Read prayerfully the following sections.

Ch. 19:17–24	Jesus, King of the Jews, is crucified between two thieves.
Ch. 19:25–27	Jesus shows care and compassion for His mother and John.
Ch. 19:28–30	Jesus completes the work of salvation by dying.
Ch. 19:31–42	Jesus is carried to a rich man's tomb and buried.

Review the passage and answer these context questions.

How many soldiers were in charge of Jesus?

Who was the man who gave testimony?

Why was Jesus placed in the garden tomb?

Research study questions; refer to scripture cross-references.

Who took over carrying Jesus' cross? What additional information can be learned of these events? Luke 23:26–32.

Golgotha means "the place of a skull," as does our English word "Calvary." Why was it called "the place of a skull"?

It has been said a person dies a thousand deaths when crucified. How do the Psalms speak of His agony? Ps. 22. John records three of Jesus' sayings from the cross. What were the other four sayings? Matt. 27:46; Luke 23:34, 43, 46.

Record your answer to these self-examination questions.

How have I acknowledged Jesus as King of my life?

How often do I let self-pity prevent me from caring for others?

On whom and on what am I basing my salvation and security?

How much of what I possess am I willing to give Jesus?

Respond to God in prayer and praise.

Ask for a deeper understanding of the sufferings of Christ.
Praise God the work of salvation is finished. Ask for more generosity in giving to Jesus.

John 20

Jesus is resurrected and appears to Mary and the disciples.

Read prayerfully the following sections.

Ch. 20:1–9	Mary, Peter, and John revisit the tomb finding it empty.
Ch. 20:10–18	Jesus reveals Himself to Mary by saying her name.
Ch. 20:19–23	Jesus reappears to disciples and commissions them.
Ch. 20:24–31	Jesus reveals His wounds, and Thomas acknowledges Jesus.

Review the passage and answer these context questions.

Why is Peter's companion referred to as "the other disciple"?

Why did Jesus show them His hands and side?

What else did Jesus do in the presence of the disciples?

Research study questions; refer to scripture cross-references.

Do you think the stone was removed from the tomb to let the disciple in rather than to let Jesus out? Who moved the stone? Matt. 28:2–4; John 20:6, 7.

If Christ's body had been stolen, would there have been any grave clothes? John 11:44. Jesus has removed the vestiges of death. How does Paul describe it? 1 Cor. 15:55, 56.

Why did Mary not recognize Jesus? Was it tears in her eyes or a complete surprise?

Record your answer to these self-examination questions.

What circumstances convince me that Jesus rose from the dead?

When Jesus calls my name, how obediently do I respond?

How do doubts stop me from proclaiming Jesus as my Lord and God?

Respond to God in prayer and praise.

Ask for a greater determination to follow Jesus. Praise God He knows us by name. Ask for more obedience to respond when called.

John 21

Jesus directs the disciples' fishing and helps remorseful Peter to recover.

Read prayerfully the following sections.

Ch. 21:1–14	The risen Christ surprises the disciples and directs their fishing.
Ch. 21:15–17	The reassuring Christ gives Peter an opportunity to recover.
Ch. 21:18–25	The reinstating Christ calls Peter once more to follow.

Review the passage and answer these context questions.

How many disciples saw Jesus by the Sea of Tiberias?

How did the disciples know that it was the Lord?

Who is the disciple who is called "the one Jesus loved"?

Research study questions; refer to scripture cross-references.

Might Peter may have lost sight of his calling when he said, "I'm going out to fish"?

On a previous occasion the disciples had fished all night and caught nothing, but on Jesus' command they let the net down again and the miraculous happened. What did Jesus say they would catch after this miracle? Luke 5:1–11.

Jesus was cooking on a charcoal fire. Of which event would this have reminded Peter? John 18:15–18.

Record your answer to these self-examination questions.

In what way have I become a fisher of men? How does Jesus direct my witnessing?

When have I expressed my love for the Lord? How can I feed God's sheep?

What does God expect of me?

Respond to God in prayer and praise.

Ask for help to become a fisher of men and women.
Praise God for second chances. Ask for grace to follow more closely.

The Holy Spirit is promised, as the disciples witness the ascension.

Read prayerfully the following sections.

Ch. 1:1–4	Luke records the resurrection appearances of Jesus.
Ch. 1:5–11	The eleven living disciples are recommissioned before Jesus ascends.
Ch. 1:12–26	These eleven men replace the now-deceased Judas with Matthias.

Review the passage and answer these context questions.

What question did the disciples ask Jesus?

Which kingdom did Jesus speak to His disciples about?

Why did the disciples choose to elect a replacement for Judas?

Research study questions; refer to scripture cross-references.

What in the opening verses leads to the conclusion that Luke was the author of this book? Luke 1:1–4.

As the resurrection body of Jesus would have needed no food, was the reason that Jesus ate with them to prove that He was not a phantom? Luke 24:39, 42; Acts 10:41.

Where in the Old Testament is the casting of lots a legitimate means of making a decision? Prov. 16:33. Was this method ever used again in the New Testament? Did the eleven make the right choice?

Record your answer to these self-examination questions.

How well prepared am I for the work Jesus has for me?

As I wait for Jesus' return, in what way has the Holy Spirit empowered me?

How does God help us today to choose our spiritual leaders?

Respond to God in prayer and praise.

Praise God that Jesus is risen. Ask for ears to hear the call of God. Ask for wisdom to appoint spiritual leaders.

The Holy Spirit comes; Peter preaches; and the church is born.

Read prayerfully the following sections.

Ch. 2:1–13	The Holy Spirit comes, enabling disciples to speak in other languages.
Ch. 2:14–41	Peter clarifies the phenomenon, and then preaches Christ crucified.
Ch. 2:42–47	New converts continue to grow as they fellowship together.

Review the passage and answer these context questions.

What were the signs of the coming of the Spirit?

Were all Joel's prophecies fulfilled on the day of Pentecost?

Why was David able to speak of the resurrection of Jesus?

Research study questions; refer to scripture cross-references.

What does the word "Pentecost" mean? When was it celebrated? Is it the same feast as the "feast of weeks" and the "day of the first fruits"? Lev. 23:15; Num. 28:26; Deut. 16:10.

What is the difference between the baptism of the Holy Spirit and the filling of the Holy Spirit? 1 Cor. 12:13; Eph. 5:18.

What might the expression "they broke bread" signify? 1 Cor. 11:17–33.

Record your answer to these self-examination questions.

How can I be emboldened to speak of Jesus?

When did I receive forgiveness for my sins?

How can I witness to others through being baptized? How important is baptism?

Respond to God in prayer and praise.

Ask for the filling of the Holy Spirit. Ask to be enabled to preach Christ crucified.
Praise God for the fellowship of His church.

Acts 3—4

The apostles perform a miracle and are cautioned by religious rulers.

Read prayerfully the following sections.

Ch. 3:1–26	Peter heals a crippled beggar in the name of Jesus.
Ch. 4:1–22	Religious leaders reject the proclamation of the resurrection.
Ch. 4:23–31	Believers pray powerfully for the apostles in their preaching.
Ch. 4:32–37	Grace-filled believers share possessions with those in need.

Review the passage and answer these context questions.

Why was this miracle especially notable?

What was the content of the preaching that disturbed the Sadducees?

What did the believers pray for at this time?

Research study questions; refer to scripture cross-references.

Did these extraordinary miracles continue throughout the lifetime of the apostles? 2 Tim. 4:20.

Peter accuses the men of Israel of killing Jesus. Was this true? Who else is guilty of His death? Is. 53:5.

Why were the Sadducees so annoyed at the preaching of the resurrection? Acts 23:8.

Record your answer to these self-examination questions.

How do I react when I see God at work in changing lives?

When faced with opposition, where can I find courage?

What is my responsibility to those in need—even when the government provides?

Respond to God in prayer and praise.

Praise God for divine healing.
Ask for courage to preach Christ and the resurrection. Ask for power in prayer.

God brings judgment upon Ananias and Sapphira as the church grows.

Read prayerfully the following sections.

Ch. 5:1–11	Ananias and Sapphira are punished for lying to the Holy Spirit.
Ch. 5:12–16	The apostles perform miracles of healing, and the church grows.
Ch. 5:17–42	The apostles are pressured by the religious leaders not to preach.

Review the passage and answer these context questions.

What was the sin of Ananias and Sapphira?

How did the angel describe the message of the gospel?

Why has the preaching of Jesus survived for approximately two thousand years?

Research study questions; refer to scripture cross-references.

In what way is the story of Ananias similar to the story of Achan in the book of Joshua? Josh. 7.

Why, despite the signs and wonders performed by the apostles, did no one dare associate with the group of believers?

Where did Peter and the apostles receive such courage to stand up against the Sanhedrin? Acts 1:8; John 16:5–16; John 17.

Record your answer to these self-examination questions.

In what way am I lying to God when I communicate untruths to others?

What is my responsibility to those who have authority over me?

How strong a witness am I when faced with opposition?

Respond to God in prayer and praise.

Ask for honesty before God and men. Praise God for the evidence of God at work. Ask for courage to face opposition.

Acts 6—7

The arrest, defense, and execution of Stephen—the first martyr.

Read prayerfully the following sections.

Ch. 6:1–7	Seven deacons are appointed to free teachers from pastoral duties.
Ch. 6:8–15	Stephen is arrested and brought before the Sanhedrin.
Ch. 7:1–53	Stephen accuses the nation of Israel of the murder of Jesus.
Ch. 7:54–60	Stephen is assassinated and becomes the first Christian martyr.

Review the passage and answer these context questions.

What was Stephen accused of saying?

Who was the main character referred to in Stephen's speech?

In what way were the priests like their forefathers?

Research study questions; refer to scripture cross-references.

Why was Stephen, like his Master before, such a threat to the temple leaders? Acts 6:8; Matt. 21:12, 13.

How did Moses find the people of Israel in his day? Were they rebellious? Heb. 3:16–19.

What was unusual about what Stephen saw as he looked into heaven? Why was the heavenly scene different from the normal? Heb. 1:13.

Record your answer to these self-examination questions.

What is my attitude toward false accusations, and how will my testimony be remembered?

How am I guilty of disobeying God's teaching, thus betraying Jesus Christ?

In what way do I show forgiveness to those who are my enemies?

Respond to God in prayer and praise.

Ask for a willingness to exercise spiritual gifts. Praise God for the Christian martyrs. Ask for courage to declare the whole gospel.

Believers are scattered; Peter exposes Simon; and Philip baptizes the Ethiopian.

Read prayerfully the following sections.

Ch. 8:1–3	Saul of Tarsus approves of Stephen's death and persecutes Christians.
Ch. 8:4–8	Philip proclaims Christ in Samaria, and many are healed.
Ch. 8:9–25	A sorcerer, who earlier professed Christ, proposes bribe for the Holy Spirit's power.
Ch. 8:26–40	Philip preaches to an Ethiopian eunuch who believes and is baptized.

Review the passage and answer these context questions.

What method did God use to spread the gospel at this time?

What was Simon's intention in offering Peter money?

Who led Philip to witness to the Ethiopian eunuch?

Research study questions; refer to scripture cross-references.

Who gave Saul the authority to persecute the church? Why was he so determined to destroy this new movement? Acts 26:9, 10.

Who else shared the message of salvation with the Samaritans? John 4.

Why did Philip and the Ethiopian need a body of water for baptism? John 3:23; Rom. 6:3–7.

Record your answer to these self-examination questions.

How would I react if I were persecuted and put in prison for believing in Jesus?

What preparation have I made to be a better witness?

How can I differentiate between a profession of faith and a true saving faith?

Respond to God in prayer and praise.

Ask for courage to witness to those who are seeking. Pray for the spread of the gospel. Pray for the missionaries sent out by your church. Praise God that the gospel is free.

Acts 9:1–31

Saul of Tarsus is converted on the Damascus road.

Read prayerfully the following sections.

Ch. 9:1–9	Saul encounters Jesus on his way to Damascus.
Ch. 9:10–19	Ananias is encouraged in a vision to find Saul.
Ch. 9:20–25	Saul is energized to preach, and his life is threatened.
Ch. 9:26–31	Barnabas encounters Paul and convinces some fearful apostles.

Review the passage and answer these context questions.

Who did Saul encounter on the Damascus road?

What sort of instrument would Saul be?

What did Saul do before leaving Damascus?

Research study questions; refer to scripture cross-references.

What does Paul say about his experience on the Damascus road? Acts 22; 1 Cor. 15.

Saul is not only called to serve by taking the gospel to the Gentiles, but the passage also states he will be called to suffer. What is said about his sufferings? 2 Cor. 11:23–33.

In the following verses, what would indicate that Paul did not commence preaching at Damascus immediately, but rather a little later, when he returned from Arabia? Gal. 1:11–24.

Record your answer to these self-examination questions.

When did I first encounter Jesus, and what difference did it make in my life?

How is God able to use me to strengthen those who are new converts?

In what way does my life show that I have undergone a transformation?

Respond to God in prayer and praise.

Praise God for the moment of salvation. Ask for a receptive attitude to God's Word. Ask for a greater commitment to the gospel.

Acts 9:32—11:18

Peter performs miracles then opens gospel door to the Gentiles.

Read prayerfully the following sections.

Ch. 9:32–43	Peter heals a paralytic and raises Tabitha from the dead.
Ch. 10:1–22	Cornelius sends for Peter, who is being prepared for a new mission.
Ch. 10:23–48	Peter preaches to Cornelius and others, and many are baptized.
Ch. 11:1–18	Peter explains to the apostles how God directed him by a vision.

Review the passage and answer these context questions.

Whom did Peter proclaim Jesus to be?

What was the message in Peter's vision?

Why did the Holy Spirit come before his baptism and not after?

Research study questions; refer to scripture cross-references.

Whose example was Peter following when he sent Dorcas' mourners away? Mark 5:40.

Cornelius was not a full Jewish proselyte but was "God fearing" and practiced the Jewish form of worship. What additional step would he need to be accepted by the Jewish community? Gal. 6:12.

This is the third time a Pentecostal-type experience takes place. Acts 2:1–5; 8:14–17. Might the laying on of hands by an apostle have been a safeguard for the unity of the new Christian church?

Record your answer to these self-examination questions.

When was the last time I prayed for someone who needed the Lord?

When have I helped others with my prayers and gifts?

How willing am I to share the gospel?

Respond to God in prayer and praise.

Praise God for His power through prayer. Ask for a willingness to change location when required. Ask for opportunities to share Christ with others.

Acts 11:19—12:25

The witness of the Antioch church and the persecution by Herod.

Read prayerfully the following sections.

Ch. 11:19–30	Barnabas and Saul visit Antioch and the first Gentile church.
Ch. 12:1–19	Herod kills James, and the imprisoned Peter escapes.
Ch. 12:20–25	God judges Herod, while Barnabas and Saul return to Jerusalem.

Review the passage and answer these context questions.

Why was Barnabas sent to Antioch?

What was Peter's first reaction when he was led out of prison?

What brought about Herod's death?

Research study questions; refer to scripture cross-references.

How did God cause the church to expand through the death of Stephen? Acts 11:19–21. Why did Barnabas seek out Saul to go with him to Antioch rather than a leader from Jerusalem? Acts 9:15.

What can be discovered about James' predicted death? Mark 10:39.

At the beginning of Peter's escape, did Peter think it was really happening? When did he realize that it was not a dream or a vision? Acts 12:9, 11.

Record your answer to these self-examination questions.

What steps do I need to take to be filled with the Holy Spirit and faith?

When I pray, do I really believe that God is going to answer?

How often do I glorify myself rather than God?

Respond to God in prayer and praise.

Ask for greater diligence in supporting the local church.
Praise God for delivering some from death and others through death. Praise God for His justice.

Paul and Barnabas are called and sent on the first missionary journey.

Read prayerfully the following sections.

Ch. 13:1–3	Paul, Barnabas, and the church at Antioch are directed by the Holy Spirit.
Ch. 13:4–12	Paul's team departs for Cyprus where they encounter Elymas.
Ch. 13:13–45	Paul delivers a message in the synagogues, and John departs.
Ch. 13:46–52	Jews denounce message, so Paul turns to the Gentiles.

Review the passage and answer these context questions.

Who instructed the church regarding Paul and Barnabas?

What led the proconsul to believe?

How did the apostles fulfill the instructions that Jesus had given when He was here on earth?

Research study questions; refer to scripture cross-references.

How many leaders were at Antioch? Who called two of them to missionary work? What were they doing before receiving God's call?

Who led John Mark to the Lord? 1 Peter 5:13. Did John Mark leave the work out of fear or because his tasks were not glamorous? Acts 15:37–39. Did he ever become useful again? Col. 4:10; Phile. 1:24; 2 Tim. 4:11.

What scriptural basis did Paul and Barnabas have in turning to the Gentiles? Is. 49:6.

Record your answer to these self-examination questions.

How can I know the Holy Spirit's guidance? What is God's criterion?

How can I overcome worldly or demonic opposition to my witnessing?

What in my message encourages people to want to hear more?

Respond to God in prayer and praise.

Praise God for the church. Pray for worldwide missionary endeavour.
Pray for opportunities to share the gospel.

Acts 14

Paul and Barnabas preach the gospel at Iconium, Lystra, and Derbe.

Read prayerfully the following sections.

Ch. 14:1–5	At Iconium, Paul and Barnabas' preaching is confirmed by signs and wonders.
Ch. 14:6–20	At Lystra, Paul heals a crippled man; the crowd hails Paul and Barnabas as gods.
Ch. 14:21–25	At Derbe, many believe; then Paul and Barnabas retrace their steps.
Ch. 14:26–28	At home, Paul and Barnabas report on their first missionary journey.

Review the passage and answer these context questions.

How was Paul and Barnabas' preaching described?

How did Paul and Barnabas describe idols?

In what way did the crowd show their fickleness?

Research study questions; refer to scripture cross-references.

Writing to these converts at Iconium later, to whom does Paul give credit for the miracles that took place? Gal. 3:5. What sort of miracles should Christians be looking for today? 2 Cor. 5:17.

The audience who tried to deify Paul and Barnabas were pagans. What does Jeremiah say about worshipping idols? Jer. 2:5; 8:19. Angels also refused to be worshipped, but Jesus accepted worship. What does this say about who Jesus was? Matt. 2:11; 14:33; 28:9; Col. 2:18; Heb. 1:6; Rev. 19:10.

Record your answer to these self-examination questions.

How boldly do I witness the message of the gospel?

What is my reaction when people try to set me on a pedestal?

What effort do I make to disciple those who are new converts?

Respond to God in prayer and praise.

Pray for power in presenting the gospel. Pray for humility, giving God the glory. Praise God for new converts.

The Jerusalem council meets on the question of circumcision.

Read prayerfully the following sections.

Ch. 15:1–5	Paul and Barnabas are sent to Jerusalem over the dispute about circumcision.
Ch. 15:6–12	Peter expounds the gospel of grace, while Paul and Barnabas testify.
Ch. 15:13–21	James proves from scripture that the gospel is also for the Gentiles.
Ch. 15:22–35	Judas and Silas are sent to Antioch carrying an official council letter.

Review the passage and answer these context questions.

What party had already infiltrated the church?

In what way were Gentile believers saved?

As well as the apostles and elders, whose authority was also alluded to in the letter?

Research study questions; refer to scripture cross-references.

What was the original spiritual significance of circumcision? Gen. 17:10–14.

Grace is God's unmerited favor. What does scripture say about being saved by grace without the need of good works? Rom. 3:28; Eph. 2:8, 9; Titus 3:5.

Does James' instruction to Gentiles regarding foods offered to idols, sexual immorality, and so forth, apply today? When does it apply and why? 1 Cor. 8:1–13; 6:18; 10:8; 1 Thess. 4:3.

Record your answer to these self-examination questions.

In what way am I hindering the work of God by being legalistic?

With whom am I sharing the gospel?

How might I make it difficult for unbelievers to turn to God?

Respond to God in prayer and praise.

Ask for help to understand grace. Ask for help not to be legalistic. Praise God that the gospel is available to all.

Acts 15:36—16:40

Paul sets out on second missionary journey and arrives in Europe.

Read prayerfully the following sections.

Ch. 15:36–41	The rift between Paul and Barnabas over John Mark leads to their separation.
Ch. 16:1–5	Timothy joins Paul and Silas as they journey, bringing blessing to many.
Ch. 16:6–15	Paul receives Macedonian call; Luke joins the team; Lydia is converted.
Ch. 16:16–40	Paul and Silas miraculously released from prison, and the jailer is converted.

Review the passage and answer these context questions.

How many teams set out on the second missionary journey?

Why was Timothy classified as Jewish?

What action did Paul take against the illegal beating that was administered to him?

Research study questions; refer to scripture cross-references.

How is God's providence seen in the quarrel between Paul and Barnabas? Acts 15:39–41.

Might Paul have had Timothy circumcised so that Timothy would have a greater ministry among Jews? 1 Cor. 9:20–23; Gal. 2:1–5.

Luke, during his narrative, changes from the third person to the first. What does this suggest? Who was Paul's first convert in Europe? Acts 16:10–15.

Record your answer to these self-examination questions.

How forgiving am I when others disagree with me? Do I move on without bitterness?

In what way do I encourage other believers?

Where does God want me to serve Him? How ready am I to obey?

Respond to God in prayer and praise.

Ask for a willingness to forgive those who have let you down.
Ask for a life that brings blessings to others. Pray for a willingness to go when God calls.

The second journey continues with visits to Thessalonica, Berea, and Athens.

Read prayerfully the following sections.

Ch. 17:1–9	Thessalonian Jews form a mob to combat Paul's successful debate.
Ch. 17:10–14	Noble Bereans receive and examine the Scriptures with great eagerness.
Ch. 17:15–34	Paul preaches message on "the unknown God" at Athens.

Review the passage and answer these context questions.

What caused the Jews to oppose Paul at Thessalonica?

What did the Bereans do that was so noble?

From where does Paul say that humankind originated?

Research study questions; refer to scripture cross-references.

What caused the Jews to think that Paul was "defying Caesar's decrees." Did they fail to understand that his message referred to a future day? 2 Thess. 1:5–10.

As a Jew, what would Paul have been taught about idols? Ex. 20:4–6. How are the beginning and the conclusion of Paul's address similar to the biblical revelation?

Paul had few converts at Athens and founded no church. Might Paul have thought his presentation was flawed? 1 Cor. 2:1–5.

Record your answer to these self-examination questions.

How does my jealousy affect others?

How well can I explain that Jesus had to suffer and rise from the dead?

How important is it to me that public teaching stands up to scriptural scrutiny?

Respond to God in prayer and praise.

Ask for faith to believe the message of the gospel. Pray for the dedication to test all teaching. Praise God that He has made himself known.

Acts 18—19

The journeys continue with lengthy stays at Corinth and Ephesus.

Read prayerfully the following sections.

Ch. 18:1–17	Paul meets Aquila and Priscilla. Rejected by Jews, Paul then turns to Gentiles.
Ch. 18:18–22	Paul leaves Corinth, returning to his home base at Antioch.
Ch. 18:23—19:22	Paul begins third missionary journey with Ephesus in sight.
Ch. 19:23–41	Paul ends Ephesus campaign as the result of a riot.

Review the passage and answer these context questions.

Why did Paul stay with Aquila and Priscilla?

How did Aquila and Priscilla go about instructing Apollos?

When would a person normally receive the Holy Spirit?

Research study questions; refer to scripture cross-references.

What clue comes from Paul's second letter to the Corinthians as to why he worked with his hands to support himself? 2 Cor. 11:7–9.

Is there a similarity between Paul laying his hands on these disciples of John the Baptist and Peter laying his hands on the Samaritans? Acts 8:1:4–16.

Many extraordinary miracles are recorded at Ephesus. Where else are similar miracles mentioned? Acts 5:15; Mark 5:25–29; 6:56. Why do we not witness such miracles today?

Record your answer to these self-examination questions.

When involved in Christian ministry, what can I do to support myself?

What do I mean when I say "God willing"?

In what way am I using my home to help others to grow in the Lord?

Respond to God in prayer and praise.

Ask for guidance in sharing the gospel message.
Pray for a desire to cooperate with other church members. Ask for the energy to keep serving God.

Paul's travels are highlighted by the raising of Eutychus from the dead.

Read prayerfully the following sections.

Ch. 20–1-6	Paul and his helpers encourage many in Macedonia.
Ch. 20:7–12	Paul restores Eutychus' life after he fell from a loft.
Ch. 20:13–38	Paul encourages Ephesians by example, and then commits them to God.

Review the passage and answer these context questions.

What did the early church do on the first day of the week?

Whom did Paul meet at Miletus?

Why was Paul innocent of the blood of all men?

Research study questions; refer to scripture cross-references.

It is generally thought that the men who accompanied Paul were taking funds they had collected for the poor at Jerusalem. What can we understand about this collection? Acts 24.

Who was with Paul at Troas that would confirm that Eutychus was certainly dead? When does the "we" section of Acts begin again?

Where in the Gospels does it say that Jesus taught, "It is more blessed to give than to receive"? What scriptures would indicate that Jesus taught this? Luke 6:38; John 21:25.

Record your answer to these self-examination questions.

How many words of encouragement are in my daily vocabulary?

In what way can I show compassion to others when they are distressed?

What is the most important task God has given me to do?

Respond to God in prayer and praise.

Ask for help to be an encourager. Praise God for new life in Christ.
Ask for diligence in doing the Lord's work.

Acts 21:1—22:29

Paul is arrested and defends himself in Jerusalem.

Read prayerfully the following sections.

Ch. 21:1–16	Paul's friends implore him not to visit Jerusalem.
Ch. 21:17–26	Paul's initial report is received by leaders, but legalists have their way.
Ch. 21:27—22:29	Paul is identified, arrested, and then makes a defense to the crowd.

Review the passage and answer these context questions.

Why did Paul submit himself to the temple purification rite?

Why did the Roman commander arrest Paul?

What part of Paul's speech infuriated the Jews?

Research study questions; refer to scripture cross-references.

Did Agabus forbid Paul from going to Jerusalem, or did he just inform him what would happen when he went there? Acts 21:10, 11.

Did the Jerusalem leaders' plan work for Paul? What was the result? Acts 22:21–23.

What was it in Paul's testimony before the temple crowd that upset them? Is the world still as racist today? What do the scriptures say about this attitude? Eph. 2:14–22.

Record your answer to these self-examination questions.

How willing am I to do God's will when my friends try to dissuade me?

How often do legalistic practices erode my Christianity?

When have I shared the details of my conversion with my co-workers?

Respond to God in prayer and praise.

Ask for a burden to pray to God on behalf of others. Pray for a close walk with God. Praise God for His protection.

Acts 22:30—26:32

Paul the prisoner is taken before the Sanhedrin, Felix, Festus, and Agrippa.

Read prayerfully the following sections.

Ch. 22:30—23:35	Paul defends himself before Sanhedrin and departs for Caesarea.
Ch. 24:1–27	Paul's defense causes Felix to tremble, but Paul remains imprisoned.
Ch. 25:1–27	Paul's defense before Festus prompts him to appeal to Caesar.
Ch. 26:1–32	Paul's defense to Agrippa is convincing, but appeal to Caesar overrules.

Review the passage and answer these context questions.

Why did Paul not recognize the high priest?

To what did Paul admit in the case against him?

Why did Festus accuse Paul of insanity?

Research study questions; refer to scripture cross-references.

What did Paul mean when he called the high priest "a whitewashed wall"? Matt. 23:27; Ezek. 13:10–12.

What can be learned about the judicial system by comparing the three accounts of Paul's arrest? Acts 21:27–40; 23:25–30; 24:6–8.

What did Paul have in mind when he appealed unto Caesar? Acts 23:11.

Record your answer to these self-examination questions.

What makes me conscious that the Lord is beside me in trouble?

How important is it to have a clear conscience before God and man?

How important is it to claim only the truth?

Respond to God in prayer and praise.

Pray for protection in all our travels. Praise God that His purposes are fulfilled. Pray for strength to answer truthfully, bringing glory to God.

Acts 27—28

Paul transported, shipwrecked on Malta, and preaches at Rome under guard.

Read prayerfully the following sections.

Ch. 27:1–20	Paul warns his escort of dangers ahead, but his warning is ignored
Ch. 27:21–44	Paul warns storm-tossed sailors to stay with the ship.
Ch. 28:1–10	Paul and crew warmly welcomed by inhabitants of Malta.
Ch. 28:11–31	Paul is welcomed at Rome and preaches to all while kept under guard.

Review the passage and answer these context questions.

Who accompanied Paul on his journey to Rome?

What was the result of the Jews' rejection of the gospel?

How long did Paul stay at Rome?

Research study questions; refer to scripture cross-references.

Paul's warning seems to indicate that he was experienced in dealing with storms at sea. What does another scripture say about this? 2 Cor. 11:25.

Today, one should not expect encouragement to come from visions. Where should one look for courage and encouragement? Is. 43:1–5; Rom. 15:4.

The Bible records Paul's escape from death. Where had he escaped death before? Acts 14:19, 20.

Record your answer to these self-examination questions.

How important is it to warn others of impending danger, even if such warnings are ignored?

Where can I find safety in the storms of life?

What can I put into practice from following the example of the islanders of Malta?

What can I learn about witnessing based on Paul's example?

Respond to God in prayer and praise.

Pray for urgency in preaching the gospel. Pray for greater attention to the warnings of scripture. Pray for all Christian missionary enterprises.

Paul teaches salvation by faith and preaches condemnation of sin.

Read prayerfully the following sections.

Ch. 1:1–7	Paul introduces himself, his mission, and the person of Jesus Christ.
Ch. 1:8–17	Paul commends the church and declares the power of the gospel.
Ch. 1:18–32	Paul lists the awful sins of humankind and the judgments that follow.

Review the passage and answer these context questions.

Who declared Jesus to be the Son of God?

What has God revealed through the gospel?

What does Paul call sexual relationships between people of the same sex?

Research study questions; refer to scripture cross-references.

How did this letter from Paul to the Romans reach its destination? Rom. 16:1.

Paul was hindered by his responsibilities from visiting the Romans at this time. When did he visit them, and under what circumstances? Acts 28:11–30.

The Gentile world fell into gross sin through gradual change. Trace the fall as portrayed in this chapter? What visible things should have revealed God to humankind? Ps. 19:1.

Record your answer to these self-examination questions.

How do I show obedience to the gospel? How did I become a Christian?

In what way do I show eagerness in sharing the gospel with others?

How often do my "little white lies" lead to much more serious sins?

Respond to God in prayer and praise.

Pray for a desire to obey the gospel. Ask for opportunities to share the gospel with others. Pray for care not to be led away into sin.

Romans 2:1—3:20

Jew and Gentile stand equally guilty of sin before God.

Read prayerfully the following sections.

Ch. 2:1–16	Paul demonstrates that a righteous God will judge all men equally.
Ch. 2:17–29	Paul declares to the Jews that the Law will not save.
Ch. 3:1–8	Paul draws a comparison between God's righteousness and man's unrighteousness.
Ch. 3:9–20	Paul defends God's judgment because all are accountable.

Review the passage and answer these context questions.

What should we remember when we attempt to judge others?

Whom does God recognize as a real Jew?

What is God's conclusion about everyone who is born of Adam?

Research study questions; refer to scripture cross-references.

What does Jesus teach about judging others? Matt. 7:1–5. What does He teach about God's judgment? John 5:22–30.

What does God require in the place of ritual or sacrifice? 1 Sam. 15:22; Is. 1:11–20.

If people refuses to hear the Word of God, will this attitude negate God's promises? Ps. 89:30–37.

Record your answer to these self-examination questions.

How often do I judge others and forgive my own self-seeking attitude?

How do my actions measure up to my words?

How do my own good deeds measure up to God's standards?

Respond to God in prayer and praise.

Praise God for His righteousness. Pray for a greater realization that keeping the Law cannot save. Pray for a turning away from self to God.

Romans 3:21—4:25

Paul defines justification by faith, using Abraham as an example.

Read prayerfully the following sections.

Ch. 3:21–31	Paul teaches justification by faith without the works of the Law.
Ch. 4:1–25	Paul proves that Abraham's righteousness was by faith.

Review the passage and answer these context questions.

Where does the believer's righteousness come from?

What place did circumcision have in Abraham's justification?

Which two groups are classed as Abraham's offspring?

Research study questions; refer to scripture cross-references.

Faith must have a working object. The working object in salvation is Jesus Christ. What does God think of human effort to work out personal salvation? Is. 64:6.

Does God keep a record of our sins? Ps. 103:12. For whose sins did Christ die? 1 John 2:2.

On what will unbelievers be judged? Rev. 20:11–15. Will their human good commend or condemn them? John 3:18.

Record your answer to these self-examination questions.

What do I have to "do" to be saved?

How can I help those who think good works are the criteria?

How am I assured that I have received Christ's righteousness?

Respond to God in prayer and praise.

Pray for a clearer understanding of justification by faith. Pray for more opportunities to witness about faith. Praise God that we are clothed by Christ's righteousness.

Faith justifies the condemned and brings peace by the blood of Jesus.

Read prayerfully the following sections.

Ch. 5:1–11	God's love offers peace and joy through justification to all.
Ch. 5:12–13	Adam's sin brought condemnation and death to all.
Ch. 5:14–21	God's gift through Jesus offers eternal life to all.

Review the passage and answer these context questions.

What does perseverance produce?

Who sinned without breaking one of the commandments?

What is the parallel between the sin of one and the gift of another?

Research study questions; refer to scripture cross-references.

What kept the average Jew under the Law from entering the presence of God? Ex. 26:33. When was this barrier removed? Matt. 27:51.

What makes a person now accepted in God's presence? Heb. 10:19–22; Eph. 2:14; Col. 2:13, 14.

What happened to every man and woman when Adam sinned? 1 Cor. 15:22. Did the death of Jesus only bring us victory over death? Or did it bring more? Rom. 5:18; John 10:10.

Record your answer to these self-examination questions.

How does my life demonstrate the peace and joy God has given?

What have been some of the practical results of my justification?

When did I first come to understand God's gift of salvation?

Respond to God in prayer and praise.

Ask for a fuller measure of peace and joy.
Pray for help to demonstrate God's grace. Praise God for the gift of eternal life.

Paul teaches deliverance from sin by yielding to the new life.

Read prayerfully the following sections.

Ch. 6:1–10	Paul illustrates availability of new life by Jesus' death and resurrection.
Ch. 6:11–14	Paul instructs us to offer our bodies as instruments of righteousness.
Ch. 6:15–23	Paul insists that we not be slaves to sin but slaves to righteousness.

Review the passage and answer these context questions.

What picture is drawn with baptism as a death, burial, and resurrection?

What should be the outcome of counting ourselves dead to sin?

To what should serving righteousness lead?

Research study questions; refer to scripture cross-references.

From the following verses, what could indicate that Paul is using water baptism as well as the baptism of the Holy Spirit for his illustration? John 1:33; Rom. 6:3, 4; 1 Cor. 12:13.

How does Paul enlarge upon the subject of offering one's body to God? Rom. 12:1, 2.

What has robbed sin of its strength? 1 Cor. 15:55, 56. From what is the believer freed? Rom. 6:22.

Record your answer to these self-examination questions.

How does my life demonstrate that I have been delivered from the power of sin?

In what way am I using my body as an instrument of righteousness?

To what am I enslaved?

Respond to God in prayer and praise.

Praise God for the new life in Christ Jesus. Ask for more grace to commit all things to God. Pray for help to serve Christ Jesus our Lord.

Romans 7

Paul relates the conflict between flesh and spirit.

Read prayerfully the following sections.

Ch. 7:1–6	Paul illustrates the Law relationship by examining the marriage relationship.
Ch. 7:7–25	Paul explains the relentless struggle between the old and new natures.

Review the passage and answer these context questions.

When I am controlled by the flesh? What arouses sinful passions?

What was the purpose of the Law?

How are we rescued from this body of death?

Research study questions; refer to scripture cross-references.

While we were without Christ, we were under the Law. How were we released from this relationship? Rom. 6:1–10.

If the unbeliever is not under the Law, what is the believer under now? Rom. 6:14.

Why was the Law so inept? Rom. 7:18, 19; 8:3. Is the following statement true, "the Law cannot save; it cannot change us; and it cannot set us free"? Rom. 7:25.

Record your answer to these self-examination questions.

To what am I still held in bondage? How can I find freedom?

How often do I find breaking a commandment easier than keeping it?

What is necessary in order to give the new nature the victory?

Respond to God in prayer and praise.

Praise God that the bondage of the Law has been broken. Ask for help to seek a fresh commitment to live for God. Pray for spiritual food to feed the new nature.

Paul teaches that the law of the Spirit brings deliverance and security.

Read prayerfully the following sections.

Ch. 8:1–17	Paul teaches freedom from condemnation in Jesus Christ.
Ch. 8:18–30	Paul teaches freedom from bondage for those called and justified.
Ch. 8:31–39	Paul teaches freedom from fear and separation to those in Christ.

Review the passage and answer these context questions.

How will our bodies be raised to life?

How does the Holy Spirit help us in praying?

What does God finally do for those He justifies?

Research study questions; refer to scripture cross-references.

Why can't the unbeliever find any lasting joy or peace? Is. 48:22; John 14:27. How do our lives become more submissive to the workings of the Holy Spirit? Rom. 6:12–17.

What kept Paul from losing heart when he was under pressure and suffering? 2 Cor. 4:16–18. Is it our sense of weakness that causes the Holy Spirit to groan? What does the Spirit do as a result? Rom. 8:26, 27.

If God did the most for us when we were His enemies, what will He do now, seeing we are His children? Rom. 5:10; 1 John 3:1–3.

Record your answer to these self-examination questions.

How often do I allow the Holy Spirit to control my living?

When are my prayers most effective? And do I exercise patience?

How do I know that my salvation is secure?

Respond to God in prayer and praise.

Ask for a daily filling of the Holy Spirit. Ask for help to reckon yourself dead to sin and alive unto God. Praise God for security in Christ.

Paul defends the character of God in Israel's past history.

Read prayerfully the following sections.

Ch. 9:1–18	Paul declares the faithfulness of God, despite Israel's disobedience.
Ch. 9:19–29	Paul defends God's method of selection using the potter as an illustration.
Ch. 9:30–33	Paul discusses the paradox of those outside Israel receiving blessing.

Review the passage and answer these context questions.

Why should we not question God's election?

How will God carry out His sentence?

What will happen to the one who puts his or her trust in Christ?

Research study questions; refer to scripture cross-references.

Who else grieved over Israel's rejection of God? Matt. 23:37.

In verse 22, the word "fitted" (KJV) or "prepared" according to the Greek, does not mean God did it. What part did man play in his own destruction? Eph. 4:18.

What is the extent of God's offer of salvation? Rev. 22:17.

Record your answer to these self-examination questions.

How can I develop more concern for loved ones outside of Christ?

When do I question God? How do I know His plans are the best for me?

When did I personally receive Christ's righteousness that God gives?

Respond to God in prayer and praise.

Ask for help in prayer concerning loved ones.
Ask for patience to wait for God's timing. Praise God the gospel is available to all.

Paul explains that disobedience and unbelief are the causes of Israel's present rejection.

Read prayerfully the following sections.

Ch. 10:1–13	Paul states reasons why Israel is presently rejected.
Ch. 10:14–17	Paul suggests the remedy for Israel's recovery.
Ch. 10:18–21	Paul shares the results of Israel's rejection.

Review the passage and answer these context questions.

Why is it important that Christ became the end of the Law?

How does faith come about?

What does God say in Isaiah about Israel?

Research study questions; refer to scripture cross-references.

How did Paul use the Old Testament to prove his point? Deut. 30:11–14.

How did Paul apply the Old Testament scripture in verse 15 to those who take the gospel to the Jews today? Is. 52:7.

What was the reaction of Jewish believers when Peter first preached the gospel to the Gentiles? Acts 11:1–18. What is God's attitude to both Jew and Gentile today? 2 Peter 3:9.

Record your answer to these self-examination questions.

When has my academic knowledge prevented me from simply believing?

In what way am I helping to reach those who have never heard the gospel?

How many times have I turned away from God?

Respond to God in prayer and praise.

Ask for a greater burden to pray for Israel. Praise God there is a remedy for all.
Pray that we may always consider the consequences of sin.

Romans 11

Paul calls witnesses to show that God will restore Israel.

Read prayerfully the following sections.

Ch. 11:1–10	Paul argues that, as in Elijah's day, God still has a believing remnant.
Ch. 11:11–24	Paul asserts that Gentiles can be a means of restoring Israel.
Ch. 11:25–32	Paul announces God's timing for the salvation of Israel.
Ch. 11:33–36	Paul acclaims the riches, wisdom, knowledge, and glory of God.

Review the passage and answer these context questions.

What has happened to the majority of the Jewish race (Israel)?

What will happen to Israel in the future?

What should we give God for His mercy and grace?

Research study questions; refer to scripture cross-references.

What did the people of ancient Israel have to do to be saved? Did their works save them? Did their circumcision save them? Rom. 4:1–16; Gal. 3:1–14.

Is it possible for Israel to cease to exist as a nation? Jer. 31:35–37. As one reads all the scripture verses concerning the restoration, is it possible that one could spiritualize them? Matt. 23:32–39; Luke 21:24; Is. 59:20–21; Is. 60.

What was God's purpose in choosing the Jewish nation in the first place? Gen. 12:1–3.

Record your answer to these self-examination questions.

How can I be assured that God's plan will not fail?

Why should I look more at my own spiritual state rather than judging others?

What have I given to God that He has not first given to me?

Respond to God in prayer and praise.

Pray for the church, God's remnant. Pray for the peace of Jerusalem.
Praise God for all His attributes.

Paul instructs justified believers in practical relationships.

Read prayerfully the following sections.

Ch. 12:1–8	Paul urges believers to dedicate their bodies to God.
Ch. 12:9–21	Paul uses love as the standard to motivate one's actions.
Ch. 13:1–14	Paul underlines the Christian's loyalty to home, state, and church.

Review the passage and answer these context questions.

How should we evaluate our talents?

How should we act toward those who treat us badly?

How should we act toward those in authority?

Research study questions; refer to scripture cross-references.

Why should Christians offer their bodies as living sacrifices to God? Rom. 12:1; 1 Cor. 6:19, 20. Who is a good example of a living sacrifice? Phil. 1:20.

What does Jesus say about loving our enemies? Matt. 5:43–48. How will our enemies feel if we return good for evil? Prov. 25:21, 22.

What should Christians do with regards to the laws of the land? Acts 24:16. Does loving one's neighbor as oneself mean that we as Christians should accept all the faults and failures of those with whom we come in contact?

Record your answer to these self-examination questions.

In what way do I demonstrate that my life is dedicated to God?

Is it easier for me to respond in "kind," or in love?

How often have I fallen short of God's standards regarding practical issues?

Respond to God in prayer and praise.

Ask for added help to surrender our lives to God.
Instead of retaliating, pray for grace to forgive. Praise God for His holiness.

Romans 14:1—15:7

Paul advocates acceptance rather than judgment.

Read prayerfully the following sections.

Ch. 14:1–12	Paul requests both weak and strong to be accepting of each other.
Ch. 14:13–23	Paul reasons that restraint is required so the weak will not stumble.
Ch. 15:1–7	Paul resolves that the Romans should seek unity in service.

Review the passage and answer these context questions.

What should our attitude be toward disputable matters?

What constraints do we place on our liberties?

Why should we accept some differences of opinion with fellow believers?

Research study questions; refer to scripture cross-references.

Why did Paul rebuke the Apostle Peter for not eating with Gentiles? Gal. 2:11–13. What lesson had God taught Peter on this very subject? Acts 10:9–16.

What does knowledge do without love? 1 Cor. 8:1, 2. Are Christians supposed to remain stagnant or are they meant to grow? 2 Peter 3:18; Heb. 5:11–13.

What two things are essential to Christian unity? Paul mentions one and exercises the other in the third section of this study.

Record your answer to these self-examination questions.

How accepting am I of those who may differ from my practices?

What areas of my life need restraint?

How often am I a dissenter rather than an assenter?

Respond to God in prayer and praise.

Ask for help to be more considerate of others' views. Ask for more love so as not to cause others to stumble. Pray for a greater desire for unity among brethren.

Romans 15:8—16:27

Paul speaks of his ministry, coming journey, and fellow workers.

Read prayerfully the following sections.

Ch. 15:8–13	Paul explains the ministry of Jesus Christ to the Gentiles.
Ch. 15:14–24	Paul evaluates the Romans while explaining his ministry to the Gentiles.
Ch. 15:25–33	Paul alludes to the Gentiles' love gifts to Jerusalem Jews.
Ch. 16:1–27	Paul concludes his letter with a greeting to his fellow workers.

Review the passage and answer these context questions.

What is the believer's priestly duty?

Did any of Paul's relatives become believers?

How should we treat those who cause divisions?

Research study questions; refer to scripture cross-references.

Jesus came to minister to the "lost sheep of the house of Israel." Who were the individual Gentiles mentioned in the Gospels? Matt. 8:5–13; 15:21–28.

How does Paul explain his ministry to the Gentiles in greater detail? Eph. 3.

Who were the men appointed by the churches to assist in administrating the collection for the poor? Acts 20:4.

Record your answer to these self-examination questions.

How do I express my hope, joy, and peace in Christ?

How does God evaluate my priestly ministry in proclaiming the gospel?

If called on, how generous am I in giving to the needs of fellow Christians?

Respond to God in prayer and praise.

Ask for the words and the example to show Christ in your life.
Praise God for the power of the gospel to change lives. Pray for more opportunities to serve others.

1 Corinthians 1

Paul teaches oneness in Christ rather than division between brethren.

Read prayerfully the following sections.

Ch. 1:1–9	Paul praises God for enriching the Corinthians in every way.
Ch. 1:10–25	Paul protests divisions in the church and suggests members preach Christ.
Ch. 1:26–31	Paul petitions proud Corinthians to give God the glory.

Review the passage and answer these context questions.

If the world sees divisions in the local church what will happen to the message of the cross?

Which of the names mentioned in this chapter should we say we follow?

Why does God call the so-called weak to serve Him in the gospel?

Research study questions; refer to scripture cross-references.

How do all other gifts compare with love? 1 Cor. 13:1.

What does Paul say will happen to those who preach another gospel? Gal. 1:1–10.

What was the Corinthians' most plaguing sin? 1 Cor. 1:29; 4:6, 18, 19; 5:2.

Record your answer to these self-examination questions.

How well do I use the spiritual gifts God has given me?

What can I do to prevent being influenced by "personalities"?

How often have I allowed my pride to take control when making decisions?

Respond to God in prayer and praise.

Praise God for His gifts to the church. Ask for help to overcome divisions in the church. Pray for humility in thought and deed.

Paul teaches that the Holy Spirit reveals God's wisdom.

Read prayerfully the following sections.

Ch. 2:1–5	Paul's preaching demonstrates the Spirit's power.
Ch. 2:6–9	Paul proclaims that the gospel is not understood by the wisdom of the world.
Ch. 2:10–16	Paul proves that the Spirit reveals hidden things from God.

Review the passage and answer these context questions.

What was the theme of Paul's preaching at Corinth?

Why did the worldly wise not understand Paul's message?

How are the hidden things of God made known?

Research study questions; refer to scripture cross-references.

Did Paul show any confidence in his own gifts or ability when teaching or preaching? 2 Cor. 3:1–6.

What powers were defeated by the death of Christ on the cross? 1 Cor. 15:54–56; Col. 2:15.

How are the three persons of the Godhead involved in our salvation? Eph. 1:13–14.

Record your answer to these self-examination questions.

How often does my fear and weakness prevent me from sharing the gospel?

Who or what gives me the ability to understand God's wisdom?

How does the study of God's Word help me make day-by-day decisions?

Respond to God in prayer and praise.

Ask for the Spirit's power in witnessing. Praise God for the Holy Spirit.
Ask for help to diligently study the Word of God.

1 Corinthians 3

Paul criticizes the immaturity and foolishness of the Corinthian church.

Read prayerfully the following sections.

Ch. 3:1–4	Paul compares the Corinthian church to an immature and quarrelling family.
Ch. 3:5–15	Paul commands them to build the church rather than follow personalities.
Ch. 3:16–23	Paul criticizes the Corinthians for foolish boasting which is futile.

Review the passage and answer these context questions.

What hindered Paul from teaching the Corinthians deeper doctrines?

What happens to the believer whose good works come about by wrong methods?

How does God evaluate worldly wisdom?

Research study questions; refer to scripture cross-references.

Where do believers find spiritual food that will cause them to grow and mature? 1 Pet. 2:2.

What are some of the things that a church should be producing in its members? Rom. 6:22; 15:26; Gal. 5:22, 23; Col. 1:10; Heb. 13:15.

What does Paul say about the believer's body? 1 Cor. 6:18–20. What will happen if believers defile the temple of God?

Record your answer to these self-examination questions.

What symptoms will I show if I am an immature and worldly Christian?

How often do I seek glory for myself instead of God?

How can I control my thoughts to make Christ pre-eminent?

Respond to God in prayer and praise.

Pray for a desire to live at peace with each other.
Praise God for Christ, the head of the church. Pray for deliverance from the sin of pride.

Paul presents three characteristics of true ministers of Christ.

Read prayerfully the following sections.

Ch. 4:1–6	Paul states that ministers must be regarded as trustworthy and faithful.
Ch. 4:7–13	Paul states that ministers must endure and not retaliate.
Ch. 4:14–21	Paul states that ministers must act as fathers with love and gentleness.

Review the passage and answer these context questions.

When will God make an evaluation of a believer's service?

What was Paul's attitude when he was persecuted?

How did Paul's life measure up to what he was teaching?

Research study questions; refer to scripture cross-references.

Why is God the only one who can judge fairly? To whom is the servant answerable? Rom. 14:4.

What was Paul's condition when he was weakest? 2 Cor. 12:7–10.

What makes Paul a good example for Christian ministers to follow? 1 Cor. 11:1.

Record your answer to these self-examination questions.

How can I be a trusted servant for God?

What should be my attitude in word and action when I am gossiped about?

How do I demonstrate the working of the Holy Spirit when dealing with others?

Respond to God in prayer and praise.

Pray for faithfulness in service. Ask for a readiness to forgive.
Pray for gentleness in dealing with others.

1 Corinthians 5—6

Paul strongly condemns sexual immorality among believers.

Read prayerfully the following sections.

Ch. 5:1–13	Paul rebukes the Corinthians for not dealing with the sexually immoral.
Ch. 6:1–8	Paul reprimands believers for taking their disputes before the ungodly.
Ch. 6:9–20	Paul reminds the believers that their freedom does not entitle them to sin.

Review the passage and answer these context questions.

What did Paul instruct the Corinthian church to do with the sexually-immoral member?

Why is sexual immorality different from other sins?

How does Paul describe the law cases that believers were taking against fellow believers?

Research study questions; refer to scripture cross-references.

Why must sin be dealt with in the local church? What is the purpose of putting someone out of the local fellowship of Christians? Is there evidence that the man in Corinthians 5 was restored? 2 Cor. 2:5–11.

What did Jesus teach regarding retaliation? Matt. 5:39–48. What did Jesus do when He was wronged? 1 Pet. 2:23, 24.

There is forgiveness for those who fall into sin, but what are the consequences for those who continually practice sin? 1 John 3:1–10.

Record your answer to these self-examination questions.

How should I feel when someone in my Christian fellowship sins?

What is my attitude to those who wrong me?

How often does my vindictiveness control my thinking?

Respond to God in prayer and praise.

Pray for courage to deal with sinful practices. Ask for wisdom in dealing with disputes. Pray for a right understanding of salvation.

Paul teaches on marriage and divorce, celibacy and service.

Read prayerfully the following sections.

Ch. 7:1–11	Paul advises the single, married, widowed, and those who seek remarriage.
Ch. 7:12–24	Paul admonishes those who are married to unbelievers to stay married.
Ch. 7:25–40	Paul argues that staying unmarried allows greater freedom to serve.

Review the passage and answer these context questions.

What is Paul saying in verses 3 to 5?

What difference does Paul make between husband and wife regarding separation?

How should Christians regard material things?

Research study questions; refer to scripture cross-references.

Some claim that Paul taught his own views on marriage and divorce rather than by divine inspiration. Did Jesus give the same teaching? Matt. 5:31, 32; 19:1–12.

Should a Christian consider marrying an unbeliever? 2 Cor. 6:14.

If a believer is married already to an unbeliever, should the marriage be dissolved? 1 Cor. 7:12, 13.

Record your answer to these self-examination questions.

What are some of my responsibilities toward my spouse?

What can I say to those who are married to non-Christians?

How willing am I to stay single if God calls me to do so?

Respond to God in prayer and praise.

Pray for guidance to all who seek direction.
Praise God for His compassion. Ask for wisdom in knowing God's will.

1 Corinthians 8—10

Paul vindicates his apostleship and warns about abusing Christian liberty.

Read prayerfully the following sections.

Ch. 8:1–13	Paul warns that our freedom should not cause the weak to stumble.
Ch. 9:1–27	Paul warns that freedom to serve must be balanced by discipline.
Ch. 10:1–22	Paul reminds us of Israel's past and warns against repetition.
Ch. 10:23–33	Paul warns that freedom must be balanced by responsibility to God.

Review the passage and answer these context questions.

Is there any excuse given for causing the weak to stumble?

Why did Paul seek to support himself?

Whose conscience was Paul considering?

Research study questions; refer to scripture cross-references.

What causes a believer to remain immature and weak? Why should a mature and strong believer take the weaker into consideration? 1 Cor. 3:1–4; 8:7, 12, 13; Heb. 5:11–14.

Why did Paul try to remain independent when working at Corinth? 1 Cor. 9:12; 2 Cor. 11:8; 2 Thess. 3:6–9.

What questions should a believer ask himself before exercising his liberty? 1 Cor. 6:12; 8:13; 10:23, 31, 33.

Record your answer to these self-examination questions.

How often have my "acceptable habits" been a bad influence on weaker believers?

How do I discipline myself so that I can be more effective to serve others?

How does boasting about the strength of my faith erode it?

Respond to God in prayer and praise.

Pray for a proper use of freedom so as not to hinder others.
Ask for a disciplined and ordered lifestyle. Pray for the wisdom to learn from others' mistakes.

Paul instructs the Corinthians about worship and the Lord's Supper.

Read prayerfully the following sections.

Ch. 11:1–16	Paul reminds men and women at Corinth about dishonoring God.
Ch. 11:17–22	Paul renounces rudeness and overindulgence at feasts.
Ch. 11:23–34	Paul repeats the revelation given him regarding the Lord's Supper.

Review the passage and answer these context questions.

What woman is independent from man?

What does eating the Lord's Supper proclaim?

Who should decide on the worthiness of the person?

Research study questions; refer to scripture cross-references.

Do the Scriptures teach that women should aspire to the office of elder or teacher in the local church? 1 Cor. 14:35; 1 Tim. 2:11–15; 3:2.

What custom did the early church practice that the contemporary church should endeavour to follow? Acts 2:42, 46.

What are some things believers should remember at a communion service? Is. 53:6; 1 Cor. 15:3, 4; Rom. 5:8; 1 Pet. 2:24; 1 John 3:2.

Record your answer to these self-examination questions.

How do I show my submissiveness to God when praying?

What practical action can I take at the meal table to show that I care for others?

What occupies my thoughts at the communion table?

Respond to God in prayer and praise.

Ask for God-consciousness when praying.
Pray for an eagerness to serve others. Praise God for the sacrifice of Jesus.

1 Corinthians 12—13

Paul explains spiritual gifts, emphasizing the greatest gift—love.

Read prayerfully the following sections.

Ch. 12:1–11	Paul clarifies that there are many spiritual gifts, but only one Spirit.
Ch. 12:12–31	Paul compares the church to a body with the need for unity in diversity.
Ch. 13:1–13	Paul concludes that the exercise of love to others is the greatest gift.

Review the passage and answer these context questions.

How important are the lesser gifts to the church?

How is a person without love described?

Why is love the greatest gift?

Research study questions; refer to scripture cross-references.

Did all of the Corinthian church speak in tongues? 1 Cor. 12:29, 30. According to scripture, what are the evidences of the filling of the Holy Spirit? John 16:12–15; Acts 1:8; Gal. 5:22–26; Eph. 5:19.

Paul asks a series of questions in 1 Cor. 12:29. What is the answer to these questions?

According to 1 Corinthians 13, what never fails?

Record your answer to these self-examination questions.

What are my spiritual gifts, and how am I using them?

How can I live harmoniously with other believers? Can I accept their gifts?

When have I treated others with disdain, and how often am I guilty of not loving?

Respond to God in prayer and praise.

Ask for help to dedicate gifts to God's service. Pray for unity in the local church. Praise God for the gifts He has given to the church.

Paul explains the work of the Holy Spirit in public worship.

Read prayerfully the following sections.

Ch. 14:1–5	Paul emphasizes the importance of teaching to edify the church.
Ch. 14:6–25	Paul establishes that praying intelligibly is better than tongues.
Ch. 14:26–40	Paul explains that restrictions must be adhered to for orderly worship.

Review the passage and answer these context questions.

What should we include when teaching?

How does Paul say we should pray?

In the context of the chapter, why should the women be silent?

Research study questions; refer to scripture cross-references.

Were the "tongues" spoken on the day of Pentecost known or unknown? Acts 2:4, 6, 8, 11. If the language spoken was unknown to the listener, did it have any value? 1 Cor. 14:10, 11, 21; Is. 28:11-12.

On what other occasions did people speak in tongues? Acts 2:1–13; 19:6.

Where else does Paul mention order in public meetings? Eph. 5:21; Col. 3:17. What causes disorder? How can one know if the message or the messenger is from God? 1 John 4:1–6.

Record your answer to these self-examination questions.

How can I be sure my words will instruct and edify believers?

What should I be doing to make my church a place where people want to come?

How do I show humility and respect for God and others when I meet with believers?

Respond to God in prayer and praise.

Pray for those who teach the Word of God. Ask for a sense of the presence of God when praying. Pray that God may be glorified in all our worship.

1 Corinthians 15

Paul deals with Jesus' resurrection and the Christian's future resurrection.

Read prayerfully the following sections.

Ch. 15:1–19	Paul argues the proofs and importance of Christ's resurrection.
Ch. 15:20–28	Paul asserts that all will be made alive through Jesus' resurrection.
Ch. 15:29–34	Paul ascertains why the resurrection is necessary.
Ch. 15:35–58	Paul alludes to the characteristics of the resurrection body.

Review the passage and answer these context questions.

How many people saw the resurrected Christ?

What would be the result if Christ were not raised?

What is the difference between the first Adam and second Adam?

Research study questions; refer to scripture cross-references.

Which Old Testament character teaches the doctrine of the resurrection? Matt. 12:38–41.

Where will the believer's soul and spirit be after the resurrection of the righteous? 2 Cor. 5:1–8; Phil. 1:21–23.

Which verse in 1 Cor. 15 answers King Solomon's statement, "Meaningless meaningless …everything is meaningless"?

What were some of the characteristics of Jesus' resurrection body? Luke 24:33–43; John 20:19–29.

Record your answer to these self-examination questions.

What proves to me that Jesus rose from the dead, and when did I appropriate this?

How often do I look forward to death? What makes me afraid?

What will we look like in our resurrection bodies?

Respond to God in prayer and praise.

Praise God for Jesus' resurrection. Ask for peace when faced with death. Ask for help to declare the resurrection.

1 Corinthians 16

Paul's final exhortations, along with thanksgiving, greetings, and benediction.

Read prayerfully the following sections.

Ch. 16:1–4	Paul reminds the Corinthians about the collection for the poor.
Ch. 16:5–18	Paul requests that the church recognizes its workers.
Ch. 16:19–24	Paul relays greetings from churches and individuals and concludes the letter.

Review the passage and answer these context questions.

Should all believers give the same amount of money to the church?

How can the service of good men be rewarded?

What is Paul's great lament at the close of this letter?

Research study questions; refer to scripture cross-references.

Which two chapters in Paul's second letter to the Corinthians set details on Christian giving?

Why does Paul mention Timothy as someone needing encouragement? 1 Tim. 5:23; 2 Tim. 1:4.

What were the connections between Paul, Aquila, and Priscilla as noted in verse 22? Acts 18:1–3; 18:26; Rom. 16:3–5.

Record your answer to these self-examination questions.

How do I use my income to help others who are in need?

How do I encourage church workers to be courageous and strong in their faith?

How often are my actions superficial and artificial?

Respond to God in prayer and praise.

Pray for a grace attitude in giving. Pray for help to learn submission to leaders. Praise God for His grace.

2 Corinthians 1—2

Paul is comforted and confident that changes of his plans will profit.

Read prayerfully the following sections.

Ch. 1:1–11	Paul finds that God's comfort produces patience and composure.
Ch. 1:12—2:4	Paul explains why his plans were changed.
Ch. 2:5–11	Paul recommends that the church show forgiveness.
Ch. 2:12–17	Paul recalls the open door at Troas but that he continued on at the call of Christ.

Review the passage and answer these context questions.

Why did Paul undergo great suffering in Asia?

What is God's seal of ownership?

What is the danger if the church is not forgiving?

Research study questions; refer to scripture cross-references.

Not all suffering is for the same reason. What are other purposes of Christian suffering? Job 1:8–12; 1 Cor. 11:31; 2 Cor. 1:3–5; 4:4–11; 11:24–33; 12:7–12; 13:4; Phil. 2:8; Heb. 12:6; 1 Pet. 1:7, 8; 1 John 1:9.

Paul had planned to visit the Corinthians. Why was Paul not guilty of breaking his promise? Why did it turn out to be beneficial for the Corinthians? 2 Cor. 1:13—2:11.

Who might this person be that Paul seeks the church to forgive? 1 Cor. 5:1-5.

Record your answer to these self-examination questions.

How does my experience help to bring comfort to others?

How willing am I to change my plans when they conflict with God's plans?

When have I heeded scriptural advice and forgiven someone who has sinned?

Respond to God in prayer and praise.

Ask for patience in suffering. Ask for guidance and certainty in change of plans. Praise God He has forgiven us.

The ministry of the Word is a treasure for the believer.

Read prayerfully the following sections.

Ch. 3:1–6	Paul claims that our confidence and competence come from God.
Ch. 3:7–18	Paul explains the new covenant with Spirit-given freedom.
Ch. 4:1–18	Paul confidently claims the hope of the new covenant.

Review the passage and answer these context questions.

What did Paul imply that the Corinthians were seeking?

What prevented the Jews from seeking the truth of Scripture?

Why has God entrusted us with the gospel?

Research study questions; refer to scripture cross-references.

Is Paul teaching by using sarcasm? Who founded the church at Corinth? Acts 18.

What is the difference between the working of the Spirit in the old covenant and His work in the new covenant? 1 Sam. 10:9, 10; 16:13, 14; John 3:5; 7:39; 16:7–11; Rom. 8:9; 1 Cor. 12:11; Eph. 1:13; 5:18; 2 Thess. 2:7.

What does Paul have to say about how this present world was created? What did Jesus have to say? 2 Cor. 4:6; Matt. 19:4.

Record your answer to these self-examination questions.

In what practical ways am I placing my confidence in God as I work for Him?

How am I using my spiritual freedom to become more Christ-like?

What keeps me from losing heart when ministering to those whose eyes are blinded?

Respond to God in prayer and praise.

Ask for added time to study the Scriptures for spiritual growth.
Praise God you have been set free from sin and death. Ask for more knowledge of the new covenant.

2 Corinthians 5—6

Paul teaches that our lives should be holy as God's ambassadors.

Read prayerfully the following sections.

Ch. 5:1–10 Paul's desire is to be absent from the body and present with the Lord.
Ch. 5:11–21 Paul desires humankind to be reconciled to God.
Ch. 6:1–13 Paul desires that all of humanity receive the message and the messenger.
Ch. 6:14–18 Paul desires that Corinthians separate from idol worship.

Review the passage and answer these context questions.

Where do we live if our bodies are destroyed?

What motivated Paul to preach the gospel?

Why should a Christian not enter into partnership with an unbeliever?

Research study questions; refer to scripture cross-references.

There are only two possibilities for the Christian in departing this world—being caught away or death. (Have you ever thought that, for the Christian, there should be no preference, for to be caught up is to miss out on walking through the valley of death and fearing no evil?) Will the dead also be caught up? Ps. 23; 1 Thess. 4:13–18; 1 Tim. 2:6; 4:10; Titus 2:11; Heb. 2:9.

How is having an unequal partnership with an unbeliever classified as having fellowship with darkness? 1 John 1:6.

Record your answer to these self-examination questions.

How is my lifestyle pleasing to God?

Have I ever pleaded with someone to place their trust in Christ?

How does marrying an unbeliever compromise my life of service?

Respond to God in prayer and praise.

Praise God for the hope of heaven. Ask for a greater desire to lead others to Christ. Ask for a willingness to be taught the Word of God.

Paul recommends personal holiness and gives reason for the previous letter.

Read prayerfully the following sections.

Ch. 7:1	Paul calls for purity and holiness out of reverence for God.
Ch. 7:2–12	Paul explains the sternness of the first epistle, rejoicing in the results.
Ch. 7:13–16	Paul is encouraged and refreshed by the Corinthians' reception of Titus.

Review the passage and answer these context questions.

What promises is Paul referring to?

Toward what should godly sorrow lead?

How did Titus benefit from the Corinthians?

Research study questions; refer to scripture cross-references.

What was the summary of Titus' report? How did Paul react to it? 2 Cor. 7:6–7.

What is the difference between godly sorrow and worldly sorrow? What does each one lead to? 2 Cor. 7:9–10.

Did Paul have an intention to take sides in the church's problem? 2 Cor. 7:12, 13.

Record your answer to these self-examination questions.

How am I keeping my body holy for God?

What situation would make it necessary for me to counsel another with stern words?

When do I bring encouragement and refreshment to those who are helping me?

Respond to God in prayer and praise.

Ask for help to practice holiness. Praise God for His chastening.
Ask for a warm heart to receive the Lord's servants.

2 Corinthians 8—9

Paul gives exhortation and encouragement for giving.

Read prayerfully the following sections.

Ch. 8:1–15	Paul instructs the Corinthians to give, using other churches as illustrations.
Ch. 8:16—9:5	Paul warns the Corinthians to prepare for Titus' administrative visit.
Ch. 9:6–15	Paul explains the responsibilities and rewards that accompany giving.

Review the passage and answer these context questions.

What did the Macedonians do first before giving their money?

Why was Paul careful in financial administration?

From where did Paul's quote come in chapter 9?

Research study questions; refer to scripture cross-references.

Is true, generous giving based on the amount given or the attitude of the giver? Luke 21:1–4; 2 Cor. 8:5.

What is the first thing Christians should give to the Lord? How much should they give? Rom. 12:1; 1 Cor. 16:2.

Titus and two others are mentioned as administrators. What should this teach Christians about the handling of church funds? 1 Cor. 14:40.

Record your answer to these self-examination questions.

How am I fulfilling the grace of God by meeting the needs of others?

What is my heart's attitude toward giving? How often do I resent the offering?

What new area of my daily life can I plan to give God?

Respond to God in prayer and praise.

Ask for a spirit of generosity. Ask for awareness of others' needs.
Praise God that He is no man's debtor.

2 Corinthians 10:1—12:13

Paul defends his ministry, conduct, and vision.

Read prayerfully the following sections.

Ch. 10:1–18	Paul outspokenly states that his boasting is only in the Lord.
Ch. 11:1–15	Paul objects to criticism of self-sacrificing service.
Ch. 11:16—12:13	Paul outlines his credentials, summarizing his service.

Review the passage and answer these context questions.

What was Paul's attitude when faced with "strongholds"?

What led the Corinthians to think that Paul was inferior?

What does Paul call a man who boasts in himself?

Research study questions; refer to scripture cross-references.

Were Paul's critics saying that Paul lacked courage when he was in their presence and that he was only outspoken when he wrote his letters? 2 Cor. 10:10; 1 Cor. 2:3.

Are human weapons or viewpoints any match against the subtleties of Satan? What type of weapons are needed? Gen. 2:7; Eph. 6; Jam. 4:7, 8; Heb. 2:14, 15; 1 Pet. 5:8, 9.

What might Paul's "thorn in the flesh" have been? 2 Cor. 10:10; Gal. 6:11.

Record your answer to these self-examination questions.

What limitations should I place upon myself when I share what God is doing?

How can I avoid being a burden to those to whom I minister?

How often do I delight in difficulties? Where do I find grace to face my problems?

Respond to God in prayer and praise.

Ask for a spirit of humility. Ask for a willingness to serve others.
Praise God for the example of Paul.

2 Corinthians 12:14—13:14

Paul shows concern for the Corinthians and promises a third visit.

Read prayerfully the following sections.

Ch. 12:14–21 Paul shows disappointment that some preferred 'super-apostles' to him.
Ch. 13:1–10 Paul signifies his third visit will test the genuineness of the Corinthians' faith.
Ch. 13:11–14 Paul signs off, sending greetings and a benediction from the triune God.

Review the passage and answer these context questions.

What did Paul mean when he said, "forgive me this wrong"?

Is it possible that some in the church were not believers?

Toward what were the Corinthians to aim?

Research study questions; refer to scripture cross-references.

Is Paul suggesting that because he preached a "free" gospel to the Corinthians, that his message is inferior to these false teachers who charged money? 2 Cor. 11:8–12; Phil. 4:14–18.

What sort of city was Corinth? Acts 18:1-4.

Is it possible for Christians to be outside the faith? 2 Tim. 3:5.

Record your answer to these self-examination questions.

How much am I willing to give to those I love?

How strong is my faith? How often do I pray for family and church members?

What should I aim for in my Christian growth?

Respond to God in prayer and praise.

Ask for a willingness to follow those who teach the Word.
Ask for a faith that stands up to scrutiny. Praise Father, Son and Holy Spirit.

Galatians 1—2

Paul reminds the Galatians that justification is by grace.

Read prayerfully the following sections.

Ch. 1:1–10	Grace is declared by Paul, who preached no other gospel.
Ch. 1:11–24	Grace is demonstrated by Paul's testimony and preaching.
Ch. 2:1–21	Grace is defended by Paul's words as he opposes Peter.

Review the passage and answer these context questions.

What does Paul call other gospels?

From whom did Paul receive his message?

Did the apostles add anything to Paul's message?

Research study questions; refer to scripture cross-references.

Where did Paul receive his commission? Acts 9:1–18; 1 Cor. 9:1.

What is the test of a person's ministry? Is. 8:20; 1 Tim. 4:1; 1 John 4:1–6.

Was Paul always a defender of the faith? What happened to turn Paul around? How did Paul view his past life? Acts 8:1, 3; 9:1–17; Phil. 3:7.

Peter had difficulty in overcoming his Jewish background and in accepting Gentiles into the church. How did God at first attempt to teach him? Acts 10:9–22; Gal. 2:12, 13.

Record your answer to these self-examination questions.

What should my attitude be toward those who are preaching another gospel?

How does my testimony show it is God who has worked in my life?

Where should I find guidance when seeking the will of God for my life?

Respond to God in prayer and praise.

Praise God for the true gospel of Jesus Christ. Pray for a greater understanding of grace. Pray for deliverance from legalism.

Galatians 3—4

Paul argues the case for faith over the Mosaic Law.

Read prayerfully the following sections.

Ch. 3:1–5 Paul argues that the Galatians had received the Spirit by grace.
Ch. 3:6–25 Paul argues that Abraham received the promise by faith.
Ch. 3:26—4:20 Paul argues that sonship is for all through faith in Christ Jesus.
Ch. 4:21–31 Paul argues that Abraham's seed inherited the promise by faith, not the Law.

Review the passage and answer these context questions.

How had Paul portrayed Jesus?

What was the purpose of the Law?

In contrast to freedom, what will the Law bring?

Research study questions; refer to scripture cross-references.

What happens to a person when he or she receives the Holy Spirit? What is the believer's responsibility to the Holy Spirit who lives in his or her body? John 3:1–8; 1 Cor. 6:19, 20; 12:12–14; Eph. 1:13, 14; Gal. 5:16, 25.

When was the Law done away with and its righteous demands fulfilled? Rom. 7:4; 8:1–4; Gal. 3:24, 25; 1 Tim. 1:8–11.

What position had Hagar in Abraham's household? Was her child a slave like she was? Gen. 21:9, 10; Gal. 4:22, 23, 30, 31.

Record your answer to these self-examination questions.

Why is being morally good not enough to give eternal life?

How does the moral law point out my sin and shortcomings?

When did I become a child of God? Do I have an anniversary or "new birth" date.

Respond to God in prayer and praise.

Pray for the ability to think about grace rather than law.
Ask for the wisdom to learn from the examples in Scripture. Praise God for adoption as sons.

Galatians 5—6

Galatians are encouraged to live by the Spirit.

Read prayerfully the following sections.

Ch. 5:1–15	Paul exhorts Galatians to exercise their freedom and serve with love.
Ch. 5:16–26	Paul entreats the Galatians to exercise themselves in spiritual fruits.
Ch. 6:1–18	Paul encourages the Galatians in restoration of the fallen and exhorts them to good works.

Review the passage and answer these context questions.

Why did Christ set us free?

How do we overcome the desires of the flesh?

What will happen to the person who sows to the Spirit?

Research study questions; refer to scripture cross-references.

What losses will one incur if one turns from grace back to law? If legalism is allowed to flourish in the local church, what will usually happen? Gal. 5:2, 3; 1 Cor. 5:6–8.

What is most important in the Christian's life: the gifts of the Spirit or the graces (fruits) of the Spirit? 1 Cor. 12; Gal. 5:22, 23.

How should Christians deal with those who have fallen into sin? John 13:34; 15:12.

Record your answer to these self-examination questions.

How will my lack of morality affect others? In what way can I serve others?

When I become conceited, how will this affect my fellowship with others?

How can I be more faithful in sharing the gospel with others?

Respond to God in prayer and praise.

Pray for the ability to walk and practice the love of Christ. Pray for a more fruitful life. Praise God that He lifts up the fallen.

Ephesians

1

Paul, with thanksgiving, lists the believer's blessing through grace.

Read prayerfully the following sections.

Ch. 1:1–6	The work of God the Father in choosing us in eternity past.
Ch. 1:7–12	The work of God the Son in redeeming us for God's glory.
Ch. 1:13–14	The work of God the Spirit in guaranteeing our security.
Ch. 1:15–23	The work of Paul the apostle in praying for our well-being.

Review the passage and answer these context questions.

What did God choose us to be?

What is the seal of our salvation?

How does Paul explain the power that is at work in us?

Research study questions; refer to scripture cross-references.

Since Paul called all the believers at Ephesus "saints," can we deduce that all believers are saints? At what moment does one become a saint? 1 Pet. 1:18, 19; 1 John 1:7.

Redemption means "to be purchased out of the slave market." Is it possible to return? What was the price paid for our redemption? Heb. 7:27; 13:20; Jude 1:24; Rev. 1:5.

Who is the guarantee of our security? Eph. 1:14; Acts 1:8; 1 Pet. 1:5.

Record your answer to these self-examination questions.

In what way am I seeking to live a life that is pleasing to God?

How does my daily walk in serving others bring glory to the Lord Jesus?

When did I discover that God has given a guarantee of an inheritance in heaven?

Respond to God in prayer and praise.

Praise God the Father for choosing us. Praise God the Son for redeeming us. Praise God for those who pray for us.

Ephesians 2—3

Paul teaches that both Jews and Gentiles are saved by grace.

Read prayerfully the following sections.

Ch. 2:1–10	Paul reminds the Ephesians that salvation is the work of God.
Ch. 2:11–22	Paul relates to the Ephesians concerning the unity of the body of Christ.
Ch. 3:1–13	Paul's revelation of Jesus Christ is through the Holy Spirit.
Ch. 3:14–21	Paul reverently prays for the Ephesians to be fully established.

Review the passage and answer these context questions.

How are people saved?

Which two peoples have God made one?

What is the mystery of Christ?

Research study questions; refer to scripture cross-references.

Is it correct to say that the church is not found in the Old Testament? If so, what period does the church cover? Rom. 16:25, 26; Eph. 3:1–6; Col. 1:25, 26.

Abraham was the founder of the Jewish race. Of what nationality was Abraham? How did he become the founder of Israel and the father of the faithful? Gen. 11:28, 29; 12:1–5; Rom. 4:1–3; 9:6, 7.

How are believers equipped to know and understand the Scriptures? 1 Cor. 2:8–14.

Record your answer to these self-examination questions.

What "good works" am I doing as a result of having being saved by grace?

How do I show that Christian unity defies racism?

What gives me the courage to approach God with freedom and confidence?

Respond to God in prayer and praise.

Ask for the work of salvation to be completed in your life.
Pray for a greater understanding of Christian unity. Praise God for the revelation of Jesus Christ.

Ephesians 4

Believers are exhorted to walk in love, unity, purity, and truthfulness.

Read prayerfully the following sections.

Ch. 4:1–6	Paul urges believers to show unity, consideration, and love.
Ch. 4:7–14	Paul upholds the idea that gifts are diversified in the church.
Ch. 4:15–32	Paul uncompromisingly demands purity in thought and deed.

Review the passage and answer these context questions.

What effort should we make for unity in the church?

How should the truth be spoken?

What happens when we become angry?

Research study questions; refer to scripture cross-references.

List the seven items mentioned that unify believers. Since "one baptism" is mentioned, what baptism does this refer to and how did this take place? Rom. 6:1–4.

Believers who died before the ascension of Christ went to Abraham's side or paradise. Does this refer to the captives that were in Jesus' train when He ascended to heaven? Luke 16:22; 23:43.

What lessons are to be learned from the sin against the Holy Spirit? Matt. 12:22–32; Acts 5:3; 7:51; Eph. 4:30; 1 Thess. 5:19.

Record your answer to these self-examination questions.

How am I showing humility and patience with those who disagree with me?

What preparation do I need to serve God and how am I using my gifts?

How can I be more forgiving when I am slandered?

Respond to God in prayer and praise.

Ask for help to be more considerate to others. Praise God for the spiritual gifts He has given to the church. Pray for purity in thought, word, and deed.

Ephesians 5:1—6:9

Paul calls for holiness and submission in all household relationships.

Read prayerfully the following sections.

Ch. 5:1–20	Paul calls believers to purity and temperance.
Ch. 5:21–33	Paul outlines responsibilities of husbands and wives to each other.
Ch. 6:1–9	Paul instructs children, parents, slaves, and masters in God's plan for them.

Review the passage and answer these context questions.

What type of things should believers not say?

In what way should a husband love his wife?

Why should children obey their parents?

Research study questions; refer to scripture cross-references.

Why did Paul warn the Ephesian believers about their spiritual life? Eph. 5:3–12.

Marriage is a divine institution for believers and unbelievers, but should a believer marry an unbeliever? Why or why not? 2 Cor. 6:14–18; Amos 3:3.

What is the promise given in the Ten Commandments for obeying one's parents? Ex. 20:12.

Record your answer to these self-examination questions.

What positive things keep me from evil influences?

In what ways am I showing submission and consideration at home?

Do I treat my employees with respect and impartiality?

Respond to God in prayer and praise.

Pray for purity in walk and talk. Pray for help to show more love and consideration to our families. Ask for wisdom in witnessing in the workplace.

Ephesians 6:10-24

The Christian defense is to be clothed with God's full armor.

Read prayerfully the following sections.

Ch. 6:10–17	Paul advocates use of spiritual armor to fight the forces of evil.
Ch. 6:18–20	Paul admonishes the Ephesians to be Spirit-filled in intercessory prayer.
Ch. 6:21–24	Paul assigns Tychicus to Ephesus to encourage and inform the Ephesians.

Review the passage and answer these context questions.

What power gives us strength in the battle?

How much of the armor needs to be worn?

How much importance does Paul place on prayer?

Research study questions; refer to scripture cross-references.

What does the armor protect physically, and how could we apply this spiritually?

How is the spiritual conflict of a believer an analogy to military warfare? 2 Tim. 2:3, 4. What three enemies do Christians face? Gal. 1:4; 5:17; 1 Pet. 5:8.

There is only one offensive weapon mentioned. To whom does this weapon belong? What weapon did Jesus use when tempted by the devil? Matt. 4.

Record your answer to these self-examination questions.

How do I appropriate the resources God has given me to fight evil?

How is it possible for me to "pray in the Spirit" on all occasions?

How can my accounting of God's work encourage others?

Respond to God in prayer and praise.

Ask for more diligence in studying the Word of God.
Ask for the gift of intercessory prayer. Praise God for fellow believers.

Paul informs the Philippians of the circumstances of his imprisonment.

Read prayerfully the following sections.

Ch. 1:1–11	Paul speaks of the fellowship and love of the Philippians.
Ch. 1:12–26	Paul states that his imprisonment has advanced the gospel.
Ch. 1:27–30	Paul sympathizes with the Philippians in their struggles and sufferings.

Review the passage and answer these context questions.

How did Paul feel about the Philippians' part in his work?

What was the result of Paul's imprisonment?

What was Paul's desire when he was in prison?

Research study questions; refer to scripture cross-references.

What things did the Philippians share with Paul in the spread of the gospel? Phil. 2:1, 2; 3:10; 4:15.

What caused Paul to long to depart this world and to be with Christ? 2 Cor. 11:22—12:10.

What do other scriptures state regarding suffering for the sake of the gospel? John 16:33; 2 Tim. 3:12.

Record your answer to these self-examination questions.

How do I pray for others? How often do "I" come first in my prayers?

When I am entrapped by difficult circumstances, how good is my testimony?

How does Jesus encourage me when I am suffering for His sake?

Respond to God in prayer and praise.

Ask for more opportunities to show love and fellowship.
Pray for the spread of the gospel. Ask for patience in suffering.

Philippians 2

Paul teaches submissiveness by the example of Christ and others.

Read prayerfully the following sections.

Ch. 2:1–11	Paul encourages the Philippians to have the humility of Christ.
Ch. 2:12–18	Paul entreats the Philippians to be humble in a corrupt world.
Ch. 2:19–24	Paul exhorts the Philippians to receive Timothy.
Ch. 2:25–30	Paul expects the Philippians to welcome Epaphroditus as a fellow worker.

Review the passage and answer these context questions.

What consideration should we give to other people?

If we want to be blameless in our work, what must we do?

Why did Paul regard Timothy so highly?

Research study questions; refer to scripture cross-references.

What other scriptures teach us that Jesus is equal with God the Father? John 1:1–4; Col. 1:15; Heb. 1:1–3. What significant act did Jesus perform for His disciples to demonstrate His servanthood? John 13:1–17.

What does it mean "to work out our own salvation"? Eph. 2:8, 9. How are we saved? Acts 16:31. How does God give us eternal life?

Where did Paul meet Timothy? Acts 16:1–4. How did Paul regard him?

Record your answer to these self-examination questions.

What do I need to change in myself to have true humility?

When does complaining and arguing hinder my spiritual growth?

What marks me as a good servant of Jesus Christ?

Respond to God in prayer and praise.

Praise God that Jesus became flesh and blood. Ask for true humility. Ask for a servant's heart.

Paul encourages the Philippians, by personal example, to strive for the heavenly prize.

Read prayerfully the following sections.

Ch. 3:1–11	Paul considers his religious past as rubbish compared with knowing Christ.
Ch. 3:12–16	Paul challenges the Philippians to press onward toward the heavenly goal.
Ch. 3:17–21	Paul compares the destiny of the wicked with that of the believers' destiny.

Review the passage and answer these context questions.

What does Paul call the men who insist on circumcision?

How did Paul become righteous?

How will Jesus manifest His power when He returns?

Research study questions; refer to scripture cross-references.

Why should the individual have no confidence in the flesh? John 6:63; Rom. 7:18.

What happens to the person who breaks the rules in the Christian race? 1 Cor. 3:10–15; 9:24–27; 2 Tim. 2:5.

When will the believer's body be changed to be like Jesus' glorious body? 1 Cor. 15:42–53.

Record your answer to these self-examination questions.

To which selfish patterns do I still cling? How can I know "self" will not save me?

When difficult circumstances arise, how can I overcome them?

How does my life reflect what I believe?

Respond to God in prayer and praise.

Praise God for the knowledge of Christ Jesus.
Ask for victory over difficult circumstances. Pray for a consistent testimony.

Philippians
4

Paul's final prayers, exhortations, and greetings to the Philippians.

Read prayerfully the following sections.

Ch. 4:1–9	Paul exhorts the Philippians to rejoice and be at peace with each other.
Ch. 4:10–13	Paul elaborates on the secret of his contentment.
Ch. 4:14–23	Paul evaluates the Philippians' gifts as acceptable to God.

Review the passage and answer these context questions.

How should Christians deal with anxiety?

What will be the result if we handle anxiety correctly?

What is the secret of contentment?

Research study questions; refer to scripture cross-references.

Where does right thinking come from? Ps. 19:7–14; 119:125–127. Which daily activity will keep the believer from sin and evil thoughts? Ps. 119:9–11; 2 Cor. 10:4–6.

What happens to those who trust in the providence of God? Gen. 45:5; 50:20; Rom. 8:28.

What spiritual sacrifices should the believer offer to God? Mal. 1:6–14; Rom. 12:1, 2; Heb. 13:15; 1 Pet. 2:5.

Record your answer to these self-examination questions.

What happens when I place my worries and anxieties in the Lord's hand?

How is my life affected by my having positive thoughts?

In all the ups and downs of life, how should I be maintaining contentment?

Respond to God in prayer and praise.

Ask for help to cast all your burdens on the Lord.
Praise God for the contentment He gives. Ask for practical guidance in worship.

Paul expresses Christ's supremacy and our reconciliation in Him.

Read prayerfully the following sections.

Ch. 1:1–13	Paul recalls with thanksgiving the redemption and endurance of the Colossians.
Ch. 1:14–23	Paul relates Christ's supremacy and our freedom through reconciliation.
Ch. 1:24–29	Paul reveals his commission to share the mystery of the gospel.

Review the passage and answer these context questions.

Where do faith and love spring from?

What place does Christ have in the church?

What position does Paul feel he holds in the church?

Research study questions; refer to scripture cross-references.

How did the Colossian church begin? Did the gospel reach the Colossians during Paul's three-year ministry at Ephesus? Acts 19:20–38. To which church did Philemon belong?

Since Jesus Christ is not a created being, does the term "firstborn" mean "first in rank"? Heb. 1:1–3.

Is it possible for a true believer to lose his/her salvation? John 3:16; 10:28, 29.

Record your answer to these self-examination questions.

What is my prayer for new believers? How can I continue to encourage them?

How do I demonstrate that Christ is reigning supreme in my life?

How energetic am I in sharing the gospel with the world?

Respond to God in prayer and praise.

Ask for a spirit of thanksgiving and appreciation for other believers.
Praise God for the supremacy of Jesus Christ. Ask for a greater obedience to Christ's commission.

Colossians 2

Paul warns the church not to be deceived by false teaching.

Read prayerfully the following sections.

Ch. 2:1–10	Paul warns the believers at Colossae to be aware of empty philosophies.
Ch. 2:11–17	Paul warns the believers at Colossae to be aware of religious legalism.
Ch. 2:18–23	Paul warns the believers at Colossae to be aware of man-made regulations.

Review the passage and answer these context questions.

What is "the mystery of God" in this chapter?

What is spiritual circumcision?

What are the basic rules of this world?

Research study questions; refer to scripture cross-references.

When or how does a person receive the fullness of Christ or the fullness of the Holy Spirit? Col. 2:9, 10; Eph. 1:11–23; 3:19.

Who is a believer identified with in baptism? Col. 2:12; Rom. 6:3–5; Gal. 3:27. In Christian baptism, how does water identify us with the work of salvation?

Do the Scriptures teach that abstinence from certain foods or drinks brings spirituality? Mark 7:6–9, 18; Rom. 14; 1 Tim. 4:3.

Record your answer to these self-examination questions.

Where do I receive the wisdom I need when worldly philosophies are presented?

What sins condemn me? How can I appropriate Jesus' forgiveness?

What value do humanistic regulations have in changing my behavior?

Respond to God in prayer and praise.

Praise God for the wisdom He gives. Ask for protection from legalism.
Ask for more wisdom in the gospel to make the issue Christ.

Paul sets down rules for holy and practical living.

Read prayerfully the following sections.

Ch. 3:1–17	Paul calls the Colossians to observe the rules for holy living.
Ch. 3:18—4:1	Paul challenges Colossian households to serve one another.
Ch. 4:2–18	Paul gives further recommendations before completing his letter.

Review the passage and answer these context questions.

Why should Christians not lie to each other?

What standard of forgiveness does Paul set?

What is the context of the phrase "make most of every opportunity"?

Research study questions; refer to scripture cross-references.

The world judges us by what comes out of our mouths. What does scripture teach us about lying? Col. 3:9; Eph. 4:15, 25.

What are some of the things that cause disharmony in the home? What attitude would help to do away with these problems? Eph. 5:22–26.

Reading through Paul's prison letters, what can be learned from his prayers?

Record your answer to these self-examination questions.

Why does my old nature keep surfacing, and how can it be controlled?

How often has my behavior upset my household?

How do I make the best of every opportunity to pray?

Respond to God in prayer and praise.

Ask for help to be more holy. Pray for grace to be more Christ-like in the home. Praise God for the Holy Spirit's help.

1 Thessalonians 1—3

Paul reflects on his ministry and receives encouragement.

Read prayerfully the following sections.

Ch. 1:1–10	Paul thanks God for the faith and love of the Thessalonians.
Ch. 2:1–16	Paul tenderly reminds the Thessalonians of his sacrificial ministry.
Ch. 2:17–20	Paul's temporary absence from the Thessalonians grieves him.
Ch. 3:1–13	Paul thoughtfully sends Timothy to Thessalonica, and he returns with good news.

Review the passage and answer these context questions.

What motivated the Thessalonians to serve?

How did Paul demonstrate his love to the Thessalonians?

What was their attitude toward Paul?

Research study questions; refer to scripture cross-references.

Is it wrong to have a Christian leader who can be admired and held in high esteem? 1 Cor. 4:16; 11:1; Phil. 3:17.

What weapon can be used against Satan when he attacks and seeks to spoil a Christian's witness? What weapon did Jesus use? Eph. 6:10–19; Matt. 4:1–11.

Why is it that Christians so seldom suffer persecution? Is it because the gospel message we present is not confrontational enough? 2 Tim. 3:12.

Record your answer to these self-examination questions.

How does my Christian testimony bring encouragement to others?

What do I share of my life with those to whom I minister?

How concerned am I for the welfare of others?

Respond to God in prayer and praise.

Ask for a greater love for Christian teaching. Praise God for those who shared Christ with us. Ask for a greater love for God's children.

1 Thessalonians 4—5

Paul exhorts Thessalonians to lead sanctified lives preceding Christ's return.

Read prayerfully the following sections.

Ch. 4:1–8	Paul teaches on how to control one's sexual behavior.
Ch. 4:9–12	Paul urges brotherly love and discretion in dealing with others.
Ch. 4:13—5:28	Paul encourages godly living as believers await the Lord's imminent return.

Review the passage and answer these context questions.

What do Christians need to avoid in order to please God?

Where will the living and the dead believers meet Christ when He returns?

How does Paul say believers should react to those who wrong them?

Research study questions; refer to scripture cross-references.

Paul seems to state that sexual sins harm others besides the participants. Who else is harmed in adultery? Who else is harmed in premarital sex?

Who does Paul say the believers reject if they ignore the instruction to live a holy life? 1 Cor. 6.

Which New Testament personality is a good example of supporting himself in the ministry? Acts 18:1–5.

Record your answer to these self-examination questions.

What practical steps should I be take to avoid sexual immorality?

How often do I meddle in other people's business? Does it help or hinder God?

What things would I like to be doing or not doing when the Lord returns?

Respond to God in prayer and praise.

Ask for power to overcome the lusts of the flesh.
Pray for a desire to help others, not a desire to hinder them. Praise God that Christ is returning.

2 Thessalonians 1—3

Persecuted Thessalonians warned and encouraged to hold to sound teaching.

Read prayerfully the following sections.

Ch. 1:1–12	Paul encourages the Thessalonians in the midst of their persecutions.
Ch. 2:1–12	Paul warns the Thessalonians not to be deceived by counterfeit miracles.
Ch. 2:13–17	Paul exhorts the Thessalonians to stand firm and hold to sound teaching.
Ch. 3:1–18	Paul requests prayer and instructs the Thessalonians to work hard.

Review the passage and answer these context questions.

What will happen to those who reject the gospel?

Why will wicked men perish?

What are the dangers of idleness?

Research study questions; refer to scripture cross-references.

Jesus spoke of everlasting life; in this chapter, Paul speaks of everlasting destruction. Is Paul teaching annihilation? John 3:16, 35; Rev. 20:11–15.

Paul teaches that there is a power that is holding back the evil one (Satan), or restraining him. Who is the restrainer? How does He work today? John 16:5–15.

Why should we not associate with fellow Christians who ignore the teaching of Scripture? What is the purpose of such isolation? 1 Cor. 5:1–5 with 2 Cor. 2:5–11.

Record your answer to these self-examination questions.

How aware am I that God has the situation in control when I am suffering?

How can I determine the authenticity of the so-called "signs and wonders"?

What temptations to idleness keep me from working hard?

Respond to God in prayer and praise.

Pray for those who are persecuted for their faith.
Pray for spiritual discernment in unusual times. Praise God there is work for us to do.

Paul instructs Timothy to refute false teachers and persist in grace.

Read prayerfully the following sections.

Ch. 1:1–11	Paul reminds Timothy to counteract the false teachers at Ephesus.
Ch. 1:12–17	Paul reveals to Timothy the power of God in changing lives.
Ch. 1:18–20	Paul repeats to Timothy the importance of holding faith.

Review the passage and answer these context questions.

What sort of "talk" came from these false teachers?

When is the teaching of the "Law" good?

What sort of man was Paul before his conversion?

Research study questions; refer to scripture cross-references.

Where did Paul meet Timothy? Acts 16:1–5. What were the nationalities of Timothy's parents? What was Timothy's attitude toward Paul and toward God's people? 1 Cor. 4:17; Phil. 2:19–22.

Which five of the Ten Commandments does Paul refer to in this chapter?

What standing did Paul consider himself to have among his fellow believers? 1 Cor. 15:9; Eph. 3:8; 1 Tim. 1:15, 16. Who commissioned Paul to be an apostle?

Record your answer to these self-examination questions.

Why should I be careful not to be involved in the New Age movement?

How does my life reveal what God has done for me?

Where can I find strength when faced with adversity?

Respond to God in prayer and praise.

Ask for protection from false teachers. Pray for a clear testimony of Jesus' power. Pray for a greater steadfastness of faith.

1 Timothy 2—3

Paul gives instructions regarding worship, church members, and leaders.

Read prayerfully the following sections.

Ch. 2:1–8	Paul urges men everywhere to give themselves to prayer.
Ch. 2:9–15	Paul urges women to dress modestly and to be submissive.
Ch. 3:1–7	Paul urges the church to elect well-qualified elders.
Ch. 3:8–16	Paul urges the church to elect well-qualified deacons.

Review the passage and answer these context questions.

Who is the only mediator between God and man?

Why were women not to teach men in the church?

How does Paul distinguish between the deacon and the overseer?

Research study questions; refer to scripture cross-references.

What are some postures for prayer recorded in Scripture? Gen. 17:3; 24:26; 2 Sam. 7:18; 1 Kgs. 8:22; Dan. 6:10; Luke 18:11; John 17:1; 1 Tim. 2:8.

In 1 Timothy, Paul speaks of women's submission in the church? Where else does he write about submission? Eph. 5:18–33. Is Paul speaking about women's authority in the church when it comes to teaching men?

Which is the only spiritual gift mentioned for the qualification of an elder? 1 Tim. 3:2.

Record your answer to these self-examination questions.

What attitude should I cast off before I come to God in prayer?

What practical things should I observe if I profess to worship God?

How does my family life reflect my qualifications for leadership?

Respond to God in prayer and praise.

Ask for a greater realization of the power of prayer.
Pray for a greater desire to obey God's Word. Ask for teachers who can teach God's Word.

Paul describes the work of a good minister of Christ.

Read prayerfully the following sections.

Ch. 4:1–6	Paul compares the preaching of good ministers with that of hypocritical ones.
Ch. 4:7–13	Paul commands godly ministers to read, preach, and teach the Word.
Ch. 4:14–16	Paul calls for diligence and perseverance in the life of a minister.

Review the passage and answer these context questions.

What is the source of false teaching?

What are the benefits of spiritual training?

How did Timothy receive his teaching gift?

Research study questions; refer to scripture cross-references.

What do the Scriptures teach about marriage? Gen. 2:18; Matt. 19:1–9; Heb. 13;4. Is everyone called to marry? 1 Cor. 7:1–4.

As bodily exercise keeps the body in shape, what exercise should be done by the Christian to keep the spirit in shape? 1 Cor. 9:24-27; Heb. 5:14.

Every believer has the gift of the Spirit and at least one other spiritual gift. When does the believer receive these gifts? 1 Cor. 12:1–13. How are the fruits of the Spirit distinct from the gifts of the Spirit? Gal. 5:22, 23.

Record your answer to these self-examination questions.

When have I sought hype rather than substance from a preacher?

Which is more important to me—physical training or spiritual disciplines?

How am I using the gift God has given me?

Respond to God in prayer and praise.

Pray for discernment in choosing listening material.
Pray for faithfulness in the work of the ministry. Ask for good stewardship in what God has given you.

1 Timothy 5—6

Paul outlines the ministry of the church to its members.

Read prayerfully the following sections.

Ch. 5:1–25	Paul advises the church in its ministry to the widows and leaders.
Ch. 6:1–2	Paul articulates the responsibilities of master and slaves.
Ch. 6:3–10	Paul admonishes those who teach falsely and who love money.
Ch. 6:11–21	Paul assigns Timothy to keep the faith and guard the church.

Review the passage and answer these context questions.

What attitude should be taken toward close relatives?

Whose good name is at stake if we are poor employees?

What are the dangers of desiring riches?

Research study questions; refer to scripture cross-references.

What do the Scriptures teach about caring for the needy? Deut. 10:18; 24:17; Is. 1:17; Mal. 3:5; Acts 6:1.

What things are more important than wealth? Why? Eccl. 2:24; 3:12–15; 5:18–20; 9:7–10; 11:9, 10; 1 Tim. 6:10; Phile. 1.

What seemingly harmless thing does Paul warn Timothy about regarding the church? 1 Tim. 6.

Record your answer to these self-examination questions.

What can I do to help those bereft and in need?

When should I show respect to my employers?

How often does my financial situation get me down?

In what way am I sharing my wealth with those who are in need?

Respond to God in prayer and praise.

Ask for consciousness for the need of others.
Pray for humility to serve others. Pray for watchfulness in the local church.

2 Timothy 1—2

Paul encourages Timothy and commends him to teach others.

Read prayerfully the following sections.

Ch. 1:1–14	Paul commends Timothy for his compassion and trustworthiness.
Ch. 1:15–18	Paul commends the household of Onesiphorus for showing loyalty.
Ch. 2:1–13	Paul commends Timothy to ensure the continuity of the message.
Ch. 2:14–26	Paul condemns the actions of Hymenaeus and Philetus.

Review the passage and answer these context questions.

What does Timothy have to do with the gift that has been given him?

How will God react if believers lose faith?

What should believers avoid in daily conversation?

Research study questions; refer to scripture cross-references.

What things does a Christian need to understand to bear suffering for the gospel?
2 Tim. 1:8–10; Luke 22:42; 2 Cor. 12:7, 8; Phil. 3:10; 1 Pet. 2:20.

How was it that Onesiphorus' household was able to minister to Paul in prison? Acts 28:30.

Name the characteristics of a good soldier of Jesus Christ as noted in this chapter.

Record your answer to these self-examination questions.

How can I keep and guard the message that has been entrusted to me?

In what way am I refreshing others who are serving Jesus Christ?

What virtues do I need to pursue in practical living?

Respond to God in prayer and praise.

Ask for a spirit of care and compassion for others. Pray for greater faithfulness in service. Praise God for the message you have been given to preach.

2 Timothy

3

Paul predicts apostasy, charging Timothy to continue in the Scriptures.

Read prayerfully the following sections.

Ch. 3:1–9	Paul charges Timothy to recognize and turn away from false teachers.
Ch. 3:10–13	Paul calls to mind his own persecution and deliverance.
Ch. 3:14–17	Paul challenges Timothy to continue in the teaching of Holy Scripture.

Review the passage and answer these context questions.

Which words sum up the characteristics of the world today?

Who rescued Paul when he was persecuted?

Why is it important to read all the Scriptures?

Research study questions; refer to scripture cross-references.

How many characteristics of false teachers does Paul list? If Jannes and Jambres were, as tradition states, Egyptian magicians, how did they oppose Moses? Ex. 7—9.

Paul's teaching was not done in secret. Whose example was he following? John 18:20.

Does the knowledge of the Scriptures themselves save us? What can this knowledge give us once we believe? John 3:18–21; 1 John 5:9–13.

Record your answer to these self-examination questions.

How can I recognize false teachers?

How often do I think to call on the Lord when persecuted?

How am I equipping myself for the Lord's work?

Respond to God in prayer and praise.

Ask for the ability to discern between true and false teaching. Praise God for His deliverance. Pray for greater perseverance in study of the Scriptures.

Paul urges Timothy to visit him and re-commissions him.

Read prayerfully the following sections.

Ch. 4:1–4	Paul exhorts Timothy to correct, rebuke, encourage, and instruct.
Ch. 4:5–8	Paul entreats Timothy to fulfill all ministries; Paul recounts the race he is running.
Ch. 4:9–22	Paul encourages Timothy to visit him, bringing friends and belongings.

Review the passage and answer these context questions.

What should characterize good preaching?

What did Paul think he had achieved in his service?

What did Paul learn when others deserted him?

Research study questions; refer to scripture cross-references.

Should an evangelist only share the gospel message when he has a sympathetic audience? 2 Tim. 4:2–5; Eccl. 11:4.

What was Paul's attitude when he thought of his own departure through death? 2 Tim. 4:8; 2 Cor. 5:1–8.

Who were Priscilla and Aquila? Which other worker did this couple help? Acts 18:1–3, 24–28; Rom. 16:3, 4; 1 Cor. 16:19.

Record your answer to these self-examination questions.

How willing am I to hear the truth taught even if it brings personal conviction?

How am I fulfilling my God-given tasks?

When have I deserted a fellow worker? How would I feel in the same situation?

Respond to God in prayer and praise.

Praise God for His rebuke and correction. Ask for help to do God's work well. Pray for more help to care for the needs of others.

Titus 1—3

Paul writes to Titus, instructing him about faith and conduct.

Read prayerfully the following sections.

Ch. 1:1–16	Paul instructs Titus on the qualifications of church elders.
Ch. 2:1–15	Paul instructs Titus to give practical teaching to various groups of people.
Ch. 3:1–15	Paul instructs Titus to warn believers to separate from sinful behavior.

Review the passage and answer these context questions.

Why must an elder meet such stringent requirements?

What two-letter word does the grace of God teach us to say?

To what should a saved person devote himself?

Research study questions; refer to scripture cross-references.

Who was Titus? What were some of his tasks? Who led him to the Lord? How did he minister to the Apostle Paul? 2 Cor. 7:13–14; 8:6, 16, 23; 12:18; Gal. 2:3; Titus 1:4.

What practical lesson from the instructions given to slaves can be learned by employees? Eph. 6:5–9; 1 Tim. 6:1–2; Titus 2:9, 10.

Does the "washing" mentioned here refer to baptism or does it refer to the cleansing that comes through the Word of God and the new birth? John 3:35; Eph. 5:26.

Record your answer to these self-examination questions.

How do my actions encourage others to know God?

In what way can I be an example to the younger people in the church?

What is my civic duty and how often do I get caught up in the world?

Respond to God in prayer and praise.

Pray for the leaders in the church. Pray for the youth in the church. Ask for wisdom to act wisely.

Paul asks Philemon to rehabilitate a newly converted slave—Onesimus.

Read prayerfully the following sections.

Ch. 1:1–7	Paul thanks God for his faithful and loving friend Philemon.
Ch. 1:8–21	Paul appeals to Philemon to restore Onesimus, a runaway slave.
Ch. 1:22–25	Paul requests accommodation as he anticipates his release.

Review the passage and answer these context questions.

What extra benefit will we receive if we share our faith?

What method is used to persuade Philemon?

What touching phrase does Paul use twice?

Research study questions; refer to scripture cross-references.

What would indicate that Christians permitted slavery in New Testament times? Eph. 6:9; Col. 4:1.

Paul instructs that if Onesimus has any bad debt that he, Paul, will clear it. Who paid the debt that we owed to God? Can any charge be laid against us regarding this debt? Is. 53:5; Rom. 4:21–26; 8:31–39.

What is the significance of Mark's name being mentioned here? Does Paul set an example to Philemon in giving Mark a second chance? Acts 15:36–41; 2 Tim. 4:11.

Record your answer to these self-examination questions.

In what way am I sharing my faith?

What should my attitude be toward those who have formerly wronged me?

What makes my home a place where God's servants would feel welcome?

Respond to God in prayer and praise.

Pray for friends and loved ones. Ask for forgiveness for those who may have wronged you. Pray for a spirit of hospitality.

Hebrews 1—2

Jesus is presented as superior to the prophets.

Read prayerfully the following sections.

Ch. 1:1–3	Christ is superior to the prophets because He is Creator and Heir.
Ch. 1:4–14	Christ is superior to the angels because He is anointed and enthroned by God.
Ch. 2:1–4	Hebrews are encouraged to heed the word of salvation.
Ch. 2:5–18	Hebrews are informed that salvation is through Jesus' life, death, and resurrection.

Review the passage and answer these context questions.

How did God the Father address His Son?

In what service are angels involved?

Was Jesus created like man or was He made like man?

Research study questions; refer to scripture cross-references.

In what way is Jesus superior to the prophets? Heb. 1:1–3; John 1:1–5; Col. 1:15–20. What did God the Father say to the disciples when they saw Moses and Elijah on the Mount of Transfiguration? Matt. 17:4, 5.

How do we know that Jesus is now seated at the right hand of the Father? Acts 2:33, 34; Rom. 8:34; Col. 3:1; 1 Pet. 3:22.

What clue is given in chapter 2 that the author was not one of the original apostles? Heb. 2:3, 4.

Record your answer to these self-examination questions.

How has God spoken to me in "these last days"?

In what ways do I drift away from the Word of God?

How willing am I in helping those who are weak in the faith?

Respond to God in prayer and praise.

Praise God that Jesus is heir of all things. Praise God for ministering angels. Ask for help to heed the Word of God. Ask for help to overcome temptation.

Jesus is presented as superior to Moses, and a warning is given against unbelief.

Read prayerfully the following sections.

Ch. 3:1–6	Christ is presented as greater than Moses in His person and ministry.
Ch. 3:7–19	Believers are encouraged not to have unbelieving hearts.

Review the passage and answer these context questions.

On what activity is the believer to concentrate with regard to Jesus?

What causes people to harden their hearts?

What is the root cause of disobedience?

Research study questions; refer to scripture cross-references.

Christ was faithful to His Father. How does He show His faithfulness to His brethren? 1 Cor. 10:13; 2 Thess. 3:3; 2 Tim. 2:13; Heb. 13:8.

Where did the rebellion spoken of here take place? Ps. 95:7–11.

How many people did God judge over their lack of resting on His promises? Num. 14. How many people exercised faith, thus entering into all the promises of God's rest? Num. 14:30.

Record your answer to these self-examination questions.

How have I ensured that the foundations of my spiritual house are strong?

When have I refused to listen to God's Word and what effect did it have?

Why is it important to be pure in my thoughts and attitudes?

Respond to God in prayer and praise.

Praise God for the sure foundation. Ask for a strengthening of faith. Pray for the ability to encourage others.

Hebrews 4:1—5:10

God promises rest through Jesus, the perfect High Priest.

Read prayerfully the following sections.

Ch. 4:1–11	Believers are encouraged to enter the rest only Christ can give.
Ch. 4:12–13	Believers are judged by God's Word and nothing is hidden.
Ch. 4:14—5:10	Jesus our High Priest enables us to approach God confidently.

Review the passage and answer these context questions.

What do we have in common with the writer of Hebrews?

What will stop us from entering the Promised Land?

Under God's scheme of things, what is expected from us?

Research study questions; refer to scripture cross-references.

What two Old Testament "rests" are referred to in chapters 3 and 4? Deut. 12:9; Josh. 21:43–45; Heb. 4:4.

Where does the believer find rest?

How does the believer strive to enter God's rest? Heb. 4:3; Matt. 11:28; Rom. 10:17; Eph. 6:17.

What were some of the "loud cries and tears" Jesus offered when near death? Ps. 22; Luke 22:39–44.

Record your answer to these self-examination questions.

What is keeping me from resting in God?

How often have I thought I could hide something from God?

When have I allowed Jesus to shoulder my burdens?

Respond to God in prayer and praise.

Ask for greater faith to rest in the promises of God. Pray for an honest heart. Praise God that He can remove anxieties.

Hebrews 5:11—6:20

God promises secure hope if we appropriate His Word.

Read prayerfully the following sections.

Ch. 5:11—6:12 Believers are encouraged to grow in spiritual maturity.
Ch. 6:13–20 God's promise to Abraham was Christ the perfect Savior.

Review the passage and answer these context questions.

Why can we approach the throne of grace with confidence?

How can we progress from milk to solid food?

By helping people in need, to whom do we show love?

Research study questions; refer to scripture cross-references.

As the date of writing was just before the destruction of the temple in A.D.70, in what way could a person crucify the Son of God afresh? Heb. 6:6.

This chapter stimulates much discussion. List some pros and cons of the doctrine of eternal security. John 10:28; Rom. 8:38–39; 2 Cor. 1:22; 1 Pet. 1:4, 5; Heb. 6:4–6; 10:26–31.

What are some of the elementary teachings about Christ? What are some of the more mature teachings? Heb. 5:11—6:3.

Record your answer to these self-examination questions.

Where do I look for help when I am in need?

What am I doing to become more mature in my knowledge of God?

When the storms of life buffet me, what anchor provides security?

Respond to God in prayer and praise.

Praise God that our salvation is secured. Pray for grace to grow to maturity. Ask for help to claim God's promises.

Hebrews 7

The Melchizedek priesthood is presented as superior to the Aaronic Priesthood.

Read prayerfully the following sections.

Ch. 7:1–10	Historical argument is presented concerning the Melchizedek priesthood.
Ch. 7:11–25	Doctrinal arguments are presented comparing Christ with Aaron.
Ch. 7:26–28	Practical arguments are presented showing the benefits for believers.

Review the passage and answer these context questions.

What was the basis of Christ's priesthood?

What guarantees the new system?

What are the benefits of a permanent priesthood?

Research study questions; refer to scripture cross-references.

Melchizedek had no recorded genealogy. Could he have been a christophany, that is, a pre-incarnation appearance of Jesus Christ? Or was Melchizedek a real man, a real king, and a real priest in a real city? Heb. 7:6, 19, 23; Ps. 110:4.

Why was it that the Old Testament priests were not able to complete the work of God? Gal. 3:19–25.

Humankind needs a perfect priest. Is Jesus perfect? Is there testimony of this fact? Matt. 27:4, 19, 54; Luke 23:15, 41, 47; John 19:4, 6.

Record your answer to these self-examination questions.

What does it mean to me that Jesus, the Son of God, is my High Priest?

In what practical way does Jesus fulfill my needs in the presence of God?

Why can't an earthly priest meet my needs?

Respond to God in prayer and praise.

Praise God for our superior High Priest. Ask for more faith in entering the Holy Place. Ask for more courage to claim the promises.

Hebrews 8—9

Christ is presented as serving in a superior covenant and sanctuary.

Read prayerfully the following sections.

Ch. 8:1–13	Christ is a greater High Priest, serving under a better covenant.
Ch. 9:1–10	Earthly tabernacle is described with its limited function and duration.
Ch. 9:11–28	Christ is a greater Mediator, sacrificing Himself only.

Review the passage and answer these context questions.

How does the New Covenant complete the Old Covenant?

What were the old sacrifices not able to do?

What will Christ's second appearance accomplish?

Research study questions; refer to scripture cross-references.

Who is the only Mediator now between God and man? 1 Tim. 2:5.

Who shares in this new covenant that God has established? Gal. 3:13, 14; Eph. 2:11–22.

The blood on the mercy seat in the old tabernacle only covered sin. What does the blood of Jesus do in the new sanctuary? Rom. 3:25; 1 John 2:2.

The word "appear" is mentioned three times in Heb. 9:24–28. Link them with the three phases of the believer's salvation. Heb. 9:24, 26, 28.

Record your answer to these self-examination questions.

How am I serving God? Am I following a list of traditions or the lordship of Christ?

Which impresses me the most, the grandeur of the building or the presence of God?

What should my response be to the knowledge that Jesus shed His blood for me?

Respond to God in prayer and praise.

Praise God for the better covenant. Ask for the wisdom to see past the earthly. Praise God for Christ your Mediator.

Hebrews 10

Christ offered a superior sacrifice; Hebrews warned against unbelief.

Read prayerfully the following sections.

Ch. 10:1–10	Christ's sacrifice is greater because it takes away sin.
Ch. 10:11–18	Christ's sacrifice is greater because it was only needed one time.
Ch. 10:19–39	Believers are warned not to follow unbelievers who willfully sin.

Review the passage and answer these context questions.

Why is there no need to offer animal sacrifices today?

What does the blood do to the guilty conscience?

Who do we need to prevent us from committing the "willful sin"?

Research study questions; refer to scripture cross-references.

What can we learn from other scriptures regarding obedience and sacrifices? 1 Sam. 15:22; Ps. 51:16–17; Is. 1:11; Jer. 6:19, 20.

How can Christians know that they are freed from the burden and power of sin? Heb. 10:14, 15; 1 John 5:11, 13.

What are some reasons Hebrew people might turn their backs on Christianity and return to their Jewish faith, which is based upon the Mosaic Law?

Record your answer to these self-examination questions.

How prepared am I in seeking God's plan for my life?

What must I do to be free from the burden and guilt of sin?

How does God help me persevere under pressure?

Respond to God in prayer and praise.

Praise God for Jesus' great sacrifice. Pray for more faith in the finished work of Christ. Ask for protection from known and unknown sins.

Hebrews 11

The writer defines faith, giving examples from the Old Testament.

Read prayerfully the following sections.

Ch. 11:1–3 The writer defines faith as believing in what we cannot see.
Ch. 11:4–22 The writer gives examples of faith in the lives of the patriarchs.
Ch. 11:23–40 The writer gives examples of faith in the lives of people under the Law.

Review the passage and answer these context questions.

How do we know that God formed the universe?

What motivated Moses to leave his royal comforts?

Were the ancients instantly rewarded because of their faith?

Research study questions; refer to scripture cross-references.

What were the dangers faced by these Hebrews if they failed to live by faith? Heb. 6:1; 10:39.

Abraham lived as a pilgrim and stranger to this world. How does Peter say Christians are to live? 1 Pet. 2:1, 11.

Is it possible to please God without faith? Heb. 11:6. How can a believer's faith grow? Rom. 10:17. Does faith always deliver in difficult and life-threatening situations? Heb. 11:36–38.

Record your answer to these self-examination questions.

How sure is my faith? What do I hope for?

How willing am I to trust God for the future?

When do I look to past examples of faith to strengthen my timidity?

Respond to God in prayer and praise.

Ask for faith to believe without seeing. Pray for the courage to follow the examples of faith. Praise God for those who have gone before.

Hebrews 12

Believers are encouraged to stay in the race, enduring hardships.

Read prayerfully the following sections.

Ch. 12:1–4	Believers are encouraged to fix their eyes on Jesus as example of faith.
Ch. 12:5–13	Believers are encouraged to endure discipline that produces reward.
Ch. 12:14–29	Believers are exhorted to abstain from sin and bitterness and follow God.

Review the passage and answer these context questions.

What should we do when we lose heart?

Why does God discipline His own?

How are angels described in this chapter?

Research study questions; refer to scripture cross-references.

How does Paul, in Philippians, describe the Christian's pilgrimage? Phil. 3:12–14. What key word is used toward the end of the previous chapter in Philippians?

What position have Christians been given in God's family? Rom. 8:14–18; Gal. 4:1–7.

Christ's blood freed believers from guilt and brought them into the presence of God. How does this contrast with Abel's blood? Gen. 4:10–14.

Record your answer to these self-examination questions.

What should I do when the struggle gets difficult?

How often do I think God's discipline is unfair?

When does bitterness cloud my reasoning and prevent me from living as God wants?

Respond to God in prayer and praise.

Ask for eyes to see Jesus. Ask for more endurance when tested.
Pray for a forgiving attitude, not bitterness.

Hebrews 13

Believers are exhorted to love, to be content, to obey, and to pray.

Read prayerfully the following sections.

Ch. 13:1–6	Believers are exhorted to be free from immorality and given to hospitality.
Ch. 13:7–19	Believers are exhorted to obey godly leadership and to pray diligently.
Ch. 13:20–25	Believers are exhorted to live peacefully and to work graciously.

Review the passage and answer these context questions.

How should we regard those who are imprisoned for the gospel?

What sort of sacrifice pleases God?

How do we become a burden to our leaders?

Research study questions; refer to scripture cross-references.

Which commandment speaks of not loving possessions? Rom. 7:7; 13:9. What does Jesus say on this subject? Matt. 6:19–21; Luke 12:15.

What is the purpose of having good teachers who preach sound doctrine in positions of leadership? Gal. 6:1; Eph. 4:11–14; 2 Tim. 3:16, 17; 1 Thess. 3:10.

How is the believer equipped to serve God? Which reference in Hebrews 2 indicates that it was a second-generation teacher who wrote this letter?

Record your answer to these self-examination questions.

How do I show hospitality to others?

What should I be praying to encourage the Christian leaders in my fellowship?

What is my attitude when I am given advice?

Respond to God in prayer and praise.

Ask for a greater desire to show hospitality.
Praise God for Christian leaders. Pray for peace in our time.

James 1

God's purpose demands self-controlled lives and selfless actions.

Read prayerfully the following sections.

Ch. 1:1–12	James encourages believers to show perseverance under trial.
Ch. 1:13–18	James exhorts believers to be in control of their senses.
Ch. 1:19–27	James entreats believers to do what the Word says.

Review the passage and answer these context questions.

What must I do to receive wisdom from God?

What happens when I am tempted?

How can we find blessing in all that we do?

Research study questions; refer to scripture cross-references.

James is a book of commands. How many imperatives does he give in this chapter?

James uses the word "blessed" meaning happy. Where is it commanded that Christians should be happy? Where is the source of true happiness? Ps. 34:12, 13; Jer. 15:16; Phil. 4:4; 1 John 1:4.

How many times is religion mentioned in the Scriptures? If religion does not save, what does? John 3:16; Acts 16:30, 31; Eph. 2:8, 9.

Record your answer to these self-examination questions.

How can I achieve more stability in my life?

How can I practice listening more and talking less?

When have I asked God for His instructions?

Respond to God in prayer and praise.

Pray for more stability under pressure. Pray for patience in listening. Ask for willingness to work.

Godly deeds are the product of true faith.

Read prayerfully the following sections.

Ch. 2:1–7	James warns that favoritism can be insulting to others.
Ch. 2:8–13	Judgment will result if we are unmerciful in dealing with others.
Ch. 2:14–26	Believers' works are an illustration of their faith.

Review the passage and answer these context questions.

What is the royal law as stated in Scripture?

How did Abraham show his faith in God?

How does faith manifest itself?

Research study questions; refer to scripture cross-references.

It's said that a legalist emphasizes the commandments he keeps while an honest person recognizes the commandments he breaks. In what other way can the sixth and seventh commandments be broken? Matt. 5:21–28.

James states that faith without works is dead. Does he mean faith must have a working object?

In the Christian's salvation who did the work? Rom. 3:21–26; 4:1–6.

Record your answer to these self-examination questions.

How often have I made my bed with the rich rather than supporting the poor?

What can I do to show love to my neighbor?

What work can I find to do that will help in the welfare of others?

Respond to God in prayer and praise.

Ask for humility. Pray that you will consider others as you do yourself.
Praise God that He has work for you to do.

James 3

True wisdom is submitting to God in everything.

Read prayerfully the following sections.

Ch. 3:1–12	James cautions against the wrong use of the tongue.
Ch. 3:13–18	James condemns selfish ambition and extols heavenly wisdom.

Review the passage and answer these context questions.

What warning is given to those who presume to be teachers?

What brings about disorder and evil practices?

What reward is promised to the peacemaker?

Research study questions; refer to scripture cross-references.

Seven things are mentioned in the book of Proverbs that the Lord hates. How many refer to the sins of the tongue? Prov. 6:16–19.

What promises are given in Scripture to those who control the tongues? Ps. 34:12, 13.

What do the Scriptures say about the devil's "bitter envy and selfish ambition"? Gen. 3:1–4; Is. 14:12–14; Matt. 4:8, 9.

Record your answer to these self-examination questions.

How does what I say reflect who or what controls my life?

When have I shown consideration to others rather than persist in selfish pursuits?

Am I a peace maker or do I sow discord?

Respond to God in prayer and praise.

Ask for the Holy Spirit's help in controlling our tongues.
Pray for help to be a peacemaker. Praise God for the wisdom He is able to give.

Submissive hearts know the true love of God.

Read prayerfully the following sections.

Ch. 4:1–6	Choosing the world causes mental and physical strife.
Ch. 4:7–12	Choosing God changes our hearts and attitudes.
Ch. 4:13–17	Choosing God's Word for our lives protects against sin.

Review the passage and answer these context questions.

What brings fights and quarrels among brethren?

Why should we refrain from slandering others?

What should we say about tomorrow's plans?

Research study questions; refer to scripture cross-references.

How does Paul describe believers who fight and quarrel among themselves? 1 Cor. 3:1–4.

James states that to be a friend of the world is to become the enemy of God. What does Paul say about a "sinful mind"? Rom. 8:5–8.

What instruction did Peter give on resisting the devil? 1 Pet. 5:6–10.

Record your answer to these self-examination questions.

Why do I get so upset when I don't get my way?

How often are broken relationships and quarrels caused by my lack of humility?

What is more important to me, to know the future, or to do the will of God?

Respond to God in prayer and praise.

Ask for grace to be God's friend.
Pray for a willingness to submit to God in all areas. Pray to know God's will.

James 5

James encourages patience in suffering until the Lord returns.

Read prayerfully the following sections.

Ch. 5:1–6	Self-indulgence and wealth can bring corruption.
Ch. 5:7–12	Suffering and patient perseverance will eventually bring blessing.
Ch. 5:13–20	Sick and sinful people can be healed by repentance and faith.

Review the passage and answer these context questions.

Who hears when the rich oppress the poor?

Who is the greatest example of perseverance in Scripture?

When is it important to confess one's sins to someone else?

Research study questions; refer to scripture cross-references.

What does Jesus teach on the accumulation of wealth? Matt. 6:19–21.

What does Jesus teach about making promises in the form of an oath? Matt. 5:33–37.

How does the story of Elijah and backsliding Israel illustrate the statement "the prayer offered in faith will make the sick person well"? 1 Kgs. 17:1; 18:21, 39, 41-45.

Record your answer to these self-examination questions.

In what things have I indulged that could testify against me?

Why am I in a hurry? How can I be more patient?

How often do I pray and fully believe that God will answer?

Respond to God in prayer and praise.

Pray for moral strength to keep a clean testimony.
Ask for patience—always. Praise God that Jesus is coming soon.

1 Peter 1—2

God's chosen are to follow Christ's example of holy living.

Read prayerfully the following sections.

Ch. 1:1–12	Peter explains that trials are to refine faith, but our inheritance is secured.
Ch. 1:13—2:3	Peter expects God's chosen to grow holy and live in harmony.
Ch. 2:4–12	Peter explains the position of God's people as they live in a pagan world.
Ch. 2:13–25	Peter exhorts God's chosen ones to follow Christ, submitting to authority.

Review the passage and answer these context questions.

How did God redeem fallen humankind?

What things are we to rid ourselves of?

How did Jesus react when He was insulted?

Research study questions; refer to scripture cross-references.

The word "foreknowledge" demonstrates God's omniscience. What does it say in Acts about Jesus being delivered over to wicked men so that He might die for us? Acts 2:22–24.

Peter states that new Christians, like newborn babes, crave spiritual milk. What, according to the writer of Hebrews, should mature Christians desire? Heb. 5:11–14.

If we interpret "slaves" or "servant" to mean one working under supervision, how does God expect Christians to act or react while working for others? 1 Pet. 2:13–21.

Record your answer to these self-examination questions.

What enables me to be joyful in suffering?

How can I live a holier life?

To what authority do I find hardest to submit?

Respond to God in prayer and praise.

Praise God for our eternal inheritance. Pray for an understanding of true holiness. Ask for more courage to witness when faced with opposition.

1 Peter 3

Peter exhorts us to be submissive to God's will in the family.

Read prayerfully the following sections.

Ch. 3:1–7	Peter expounds upon the responsibilities of husbands and wives.
Ch. 3:8–22	Peter explains that suffering for doing good testifies of Jesus.

Review the passage and answer these context questions.

In what way can a husband be won for Christ?

Where should a woman's real beauty come from?

In what way should we give witness of our faith?

Research study questions; refer to scripture cross-references.

Where do scriptures speak that wives are to submit to their husbands as to the Lord? In what areas are they to be submissive? What keeps a Christian husband from taking advantage of his wife? Eph. 5:22–33.

There was no judgment for the eight people in Noah's ark. What does Romans 8 say about the believer and condemnation? Rom. 8:1.

What is Peter trying to illustrate by mentioning Noah, baptism, water, and the resurrection of Christ?

Record your answer to these self-examination questions.

In what ways am I showing submission and consideration to members of my family?

When have I given an answer that hurts, and how can I change my attitudes?

Am I prepared to explain my hope in eternal life through Christ?

Respond to God in prayer and praise.

Pray for more help to follow the advice given.
Pray for help to think before speaking. Praise God for His patience.

1 Peter 4—5

Peter exhorts believers to be submissive to God's will in the church.

Read prayerfully the following sections.

Ch. 4:1–11	Peter says to emulate Jesus by self-control and brotherly love.
Ch. 4:12–19	Peter encourages us to rejoice in suffering.
Ch. 5:1–14	Elders are elected, and the young are told they should be submissive.

Review the passage and answer these context questions.

Why should we be clear-minded and self-controlled?

What blessing is ours when we suffer for Christ?

Why should we cast all our anxiety on the Lord?

Research study questions; refer to scripture cross-references.

From the first section of chapter 4, list some things Christians should not do and some of the things they should do.

What questions should a Christian be asking when going through suffering? Heb. 12:4–11; 1 Pet. 1:6–9.

The "crown of glory" is mentioned. Name other "crowns" mentioned in the New Testament and for whom they are designated? Phil. 4:1; 2 Tim. 4:7, 8; 1 Thess. 2:19; Jam. 1:12.

Record your answer to these self-examination questions.

How do I react when I am slandered?

How should suffering bring me closer to God?

What sins hinder me from loving others more deeply?

Respond to God in prayer and praise.

Pray for grace not to retaliate when provoked. Praise God we can identify with Jesus in suffering. Praise God for the example of Jesus.

2 Peter

1

Peter identifies Jesus as the Son of God through eyewitness and Scripture.

Read prayerfully the following sections.

Ch. 1:1–4	God's grace arms believers against worldly corruption.
Ch. 1:5–11	God's power accords believers participation in Jesus' return.
Ch. 1:12–21	Prophecies and eyewitnesses testify to Jesus' majesty.

Review the passage and answer these context questions.

How do we receive "everything we need in life and godliness"?

What will keep us from being ineffective and unproductive?

Why is it important to heed what the Bible says?

Research study questions; refer to scripture cross-references.

The words in verses 5–7 have been called "the chorus of seven." What is the meaning of each word?

When did Peter hear the voice from heaven declaring that Jesus was God's Son? Matt. 17:1–8.

What is the principle of the inspiration of Scripture? 2 Tim. 3:16; 2 Pet. 3:15.

Record your answer to these self-examination questions.

What helps me when the world tempts?

What effort am I making to increase in faith?

How do I know that Jesus is Lord?

Respond to God in prayer and praise.

Praise God for His promises. Pray for a daily strengthening of faith.
Ask for the Holy Spirit's help to understand God's Word.

2 Peter 2—3

Peter calls for diligence as apostates deny the Second Advent.

Read prayerfully the following sections.

Ch. 2:1–22	Peter warns about false prophets, exposing their methods.
Ch. 3:1–18	Peter writes to remind believers of the promised "day of the Lord."

Review the passage and answer these context questions.

What sort of stories do false teachers tell?

What type of punishment awaits false teachers?

What will the new heavens and the new earth be called?

Research study questions; refer to scripture cross-references.

Noah and other patriarchs were not delivered from disaster, but they were delivered through disaster. What delivered them? Heb. 11:7.

What prophet states that the promise of Christ's return is true and not false? Hab. 2:3.

How does Peter regard Paul's writings? 2 Pet. 3:16.

Record your answer to these self-examination questions.

How can I learn to identify false teachers?

How easily am I enticed by plausible-sounding words and exciting stories?

In what way does my life show that Jesus is coming?

Respond to God in prayer and praise.

Ask for wisdom to identify false teaching. Pray for protection against false enticements. Praise God that Jesus is coming.

I John 1:1—2 :27

John declares that God is Light; advocates brotherly love; and warns against antichrists.

Read prayerfully the following sections.

Ch. 1:1–10	John declares that God is Light so we must not walk in darkness.
Ch. 2:1–14	John describes true obedience as brotherly love.
Ch. 2:15–27	John decries antichrists and warns believers against being led astray.

Review the passage and answer these context questions.

Why was John qualified to teach the subjects he taught?

What things will the believer find in the world?

Is it possible to deny Jesus Christ and still believe in God the Father?

Research study questions; refer to scripture cross-references.

Where else do we read that Jesus come from God and was God in the flesh? John 1:1–18.

What illustrations are given in the New Testament that would indicate a believer is in fellowship with God? Rom. 13:14; Gal. 5:16; Eph. 5:18; 1 John 1:7, 9.

What might the following scripture references suggest about the far-reaching effects of Christ's death? Rom. 5:6; 2 Cor. 5:14; 1 Tim. 2:6; Heb. 2:9; 1 John 2:2.

Record your answer to these self-examination questions.

How am I showing that I am walking in the light and not living a lie?

What stops me from obeying God's commands?

How can I be more diligent in studying God's Word?

Respond to God in prayer and praise.

Pray for more grace to walk in the light.
Pray for holiness that produces right conduct. Pray for right priorities.

1 John 2:28—3:24

John declares that God is Righteous and commands brotherly love.

Read prayerfully the following sections.

Ch. 2:28—3:3	God's righteousness enables us to be His children.
Ch. 3:4–10	God's righteousness protects us from sinning.
Ch. 3:11–24	God's righteousness commands us to love our brother.

Review the passage and answer these context questions.

If a person continues to sin what can be concluded?

Why did Cain murder his brother Abel?

In what way does God expect us to show our love to each other?

Research study questions; refer to scripture cross-references.

What motivated Abel to offer the right sacrifice to God? Heb. 11:4.

What motivated Cain? Gen. 4:2–5.

What did Jesus say were the greatest commandments? Matt. 22:37–40.

What statements does John make that gives assurance to believers that God now abides in every Christian? 1 John 2:20; 3:24; 4:13.

Record your answer to these self-examination questions.

How often have I thanked God that I am His child?

Is sin part of my life? How can I overcome?

What have I done for those in need? How willingly do I give?

Respond to God in prayer and praise.

Praise God that He has called us His children.
Ask for help to resist sin. Pray for a desire to give willingly in love.

1 John 4

John declares that God is Love and that whoever lives in love lives in God.

Read prayerfully the following sections.

Ch. 4:1–6	God's love is greater than the world, strengthening us to overcome.
Ch. 4:7–16	God's love is made perfect in us through Jesus' atoning sacrifice.
Ch. 4:17–21	God's love casts out fear, giving us confidence.

Review the passage and answer these context questions.

How do we distinguish between true and false prophets?

How did God show His love to us?

How can we show our love for God?

Research study questions; refer to scripture cross-references.

In what repetitive way does John address his readers in this chapter?

In what way is God revealed to us? Ps. 19:1–6; John 14:8, 9; 12:44, 45; Rom. 1:20; Col. 1:15; 1 John 4:12.

Which "day of judgment" will the believer face? Rom. 14:10; 2 Cor. 5:10; 1 John 4:17.

Record your answer to these self-examination questions.

What encouragement does God give me when worldly problems become too great to bear?

How would the world be different if I loved others as God loves me?

Why am I afraid? What prevents me from having true confidence in God?

Respond to God in prayer and praise.

Praise God that Jesus has overcome the world. Praise God for Jesus Christ our Savior. Ask for help to love others and trust in God.

John declares that God gives eternal life through Jesus Christ.

Read prayerfully the following sections.

Ch. 5:1–5	God's love is seen in us by our obedience to His commandments.
Ch. 5:6–12	God's Spirit in us verifies our eternal life through Jesus.
Ch. 5:13–21	God's gift of eternal life to us opens the door of communication.

Review the passage and answer these context questions.

How is a person born of God?

What do we call God if we reject His testimony about Jesus?

If we pray in God's will, what can we expect?

Research study questions; refer to scripture cross-references.

Is the Christian lifestyle too difficult for the average person? Matt. 11:28–30; 1 John 5:3, 4.

What three things does water illustrate throughout Scripture? Is. 55:1; John 7:38, 39; Eph. 5:26; Titus 3:5; Rev. 22:17.

What example in the New Testament is there of a sin that leads to death? Acts 5:1–11.

Record your answer to these self-examination questions.

How many times have I grieved God by my disobedience?

What have I done to receive eternal life?

How can I pray more effectively?

Respond to God in prayer and praise.

Ask for an obedient spirit. Praise God that we can know we have eternal life. Ask for more confidence in prayer.

2 & 3 John

John writes letters of warning to friends in the truth.

Read prayerfully the following sections.

2 John 1:1–13	John warns of many deceivers who deny the humanity of Christ.
3 John 1:1–8	John gives thanks for those who show loving hospitality.
3 John 1:9–14	John warns of self-centered Diotrephes and commends Demetrius.

Review the passage and answer these context questions.

John was reminding the lady of which command?

What are we guilty of if we welcome the false teacher?

What did Diotrephes love?

Research study questions; refer to scripture cross-references.

Should Christians welcome false teachers into their homes? 1 Tim. 5:22.

Gaius was a common name. Is there any evidence to link him with any of those of the same name mentioned by Paul? Acts 20:4; Rom. 16:23; 1 Cor. 1:14.

Do Christians have any right to interfere in the affairs of other churches? Why was John able to do so?

Record your answer to these self-examination questions.

How bravely do I witness my faith to others?

How do I use my home to minister to others within the church?

How often do people speak of my truthfulness?

Respond to God in prayer and praise.

Praise God for the man Christ Jesus. Ask for conviction to be more hospitable. Ask for help to not be self-centered.

Jude warns and instructs believers as he describes apostates.

Read prayerfully the following sections.

Ch. 1:1–19	Jude calls on believers to defend the faith against apostate leaders.
Ch. 1:20–23	Jude advocates growth in patience and prayer to counteract false teachers.
Ch. 1:24–25	Jude commits believers to the only glorious and powerful God.

Review the passage and answer these context questions.

What steps should be taken when godless men take control?

Why did these godless leaders use flattery?

What should our attitude be to the genuine doubter?

Research study questions; refer to scripture cross-references.

What was the sin of God's people in the wilderness that prevented them from entering the Promised Land? Num. 14:26–35; Heb. 4:6.

Why might there have been a dispute between the devil and Michael over the body of Moses? Deut. 34:5, 6; Matt. 17:3; Rev. 11:1–11.

Who was Enoch? How did God reward him for his godly walk? Gen. 5:21–24; Heb. 11:5.

Record your answer to these self-examination questions.

How can I be sure that the teaching I hear is not false?

What steps am I taking so that I can grow in faith, prayer, and love?

How can I help others to be saved?

Respond to God in prayer and praise.

**Pray for strength to stand fast against false teaching.
Ask for wisdom in handling difficult situations. Praise God that He is all-powerful.**

Revelation 1

Blessings promised as John introduces the revelation he has received.

Read prayerfully the following sections.

Ch. 1:1–3 John assures blessing to those who heed this revelation of Jesus Christ.
Ch. 1:4–8 John acclaims Jesus, His work of salvation, and His return.
Ch. 1:9–20 John announces his vision on Patmos, his reaction, and his commissioning.

Review the passage and answer these context questions.

To whom is the opening doxology addressed?

Which person of the Godhead is described in verse 8?

Who holds the keys of death and Hades?

Research study questions; refer to scripture cross-references.

There are seven blessings mentioned in the book of Revelation, the first is found in chapter one. What are the other six? Rev. 14:13; 16:15; 19:9; 20:6; 22:7; 22:14.

What two Old Testament prophets speak of the events of verse seven? Dan. 7:13; Zech. 12:10 Might modern communications be the answer to how "every eye will see Him" at the Second Advent?

By comparing verse 8 with verses 17–18, what conclusion can be drawn concerning the deity of Christ?

Record your answer to these self-examination questions.

What action am I taking to appropriate the blessings promised?

When did I realize that becoming a Christian also made me a priest?

What picture do I have of Jesus Christ as He serves as my High Priest in heaven?

Respond to God in prayer and praise.

Pray for a greater desire to read, hear, and heed God's word. Praise God for the glorified Lord Jesus. Pray for a greater desire to be led by the Holy Spirit.

Revelation 2—3

The Lord's appraisal of seven churches, whose conditions mirror today.

Read prayerfully the following sections.

Ch. 2:1–11	Appraisal of churches at Ephesus/Smyrna: gives no criticism of suffering Smyrna.
Ch. 2:12–29	Appraisal of churches at Pergamum/Thyatira: both are warned about evil prophets.
Ch. 3:1–13	Appraisal of churches at Sardis/Philadelphia: both are told that God will deliver.
Ch. 3:14–22	Appraisal of church at Laodicea, inviting individuals to repent.

Review the passage and answer these context questions.

Was there a limit to the persecution that Smyrna would suffer?

What was the church at Thyatira commended?

Whom does Jesus rebuke and discipline?

Research study questions; refer to scripture cross-references.

What is understood by the term "the second death"? When and where will this judgment take place? Rev. 20:11–15.

What led Balaam the prophet to fall into false teaching? 2 Pet. 2:15; Jude 1:11.

What guidelines should be considered if God has opened a door for us to serve Him? 1 Cor. 16:9; 2 Cor. 2:12, 13; Col. 4:2, 3.

Record your answer to these self-examination questions.

In what ways have I left my first love?

How can I help to restore those who fall into sin?

What is missing from my Christian service?

Respond to God in prayer and praise.

Pray for greater faithfulness in suffering. Pray for greater watchfulness in evil days. Pray for greater steadfastness in preaching the gospel.

Revelation 4—5

John witnesses heavenly events that will have consequences on earth.

Read prayerfully the following sections.

Ch. 4:1–11	John sees God's throne surrounded by praising angels.
Ch. 5:1–14	John sees the Lamb, who alone was worthy to open the scroll.

Review the passage and answer these context questions.

Was John told when these things would take place?

Who was found worthy to open the seals?

Whom did the elders fall down and worship?

Research study questions; refer to scripture cross-references.

How does the sign of the rainbow speak of the grace of God? Gen. 9:12–16. Where, after chapters two and three, is the church mentioned again in the book of Revelation? Rev. 22:16. Would it indicate that the church was absent in the tribulation period?

What phrase in the church's best-known prayer calls for the events of chapter five to take place? Matt. 6:10.

This chapter discloses that the Lord Jesus Christ accomplished the complete work of salvation. Regarding our salvation, is there any work left for us to do? Eph. 2:8, 9.

Record your answer to these self-examination questions.

How well do I follow heaven's example when it comes to worship?

What prayers of mine are in the golden bowl?

How often do I pray for Christians who are persecuted in other countries?

Respond to God in prayer and praise.

Praise God for His throne in heaven. Praise God for the Lamb who is worthy. Ask for a heart full of praise and thanksgiving.

Revelation 6:1—8:5

Content of seven seals revealed as judgment falls on unbelievers.

Read prayerfully the following sections.

Ch. 6:1–17	Six seals are opened, summarizing a time of great tribulation.
Ch. 7:1–17	Sealed are 144,000; plus an innumberable number that are praising God.
Ch. 8:1–5	Seventh seal is opened, hearlding a deepening time of tribulation.

Review the passage and answer these context questions.

How long will those slain for the sake of the gospel have to wait?

How many were sealed along with the 144,000?

What will the Shepherd do for His sheep in the hereafter?

Research study questions; refer to scripture cross-references.

Where did Jesus give instructions to believers regarding what to do when these natural disasters take place? Mark 13. What does Paul call this time of disaster? 1 Thess. 5:1–11.

When were the "great multitude that no man could count" (that John saw in heaven) evangelized and converted? Rev. 7:13, 14.

What did Jesus teach would happened to those who did not help or care for God's people in the judgment of the nations? Matt. 25:31–46.

Record your answer to these self-examination questions.

How often do I warn others of impending judgment?

When did I know for certain that heaven is my home?

How often do I pray for the salvation of others?

Respond to God in prayer and praise.

Pray for more urgency in teaching the gospel. Praise God for the saints already in heaven. Ask for the salvation of loved ones.

Revelation 8:6—11:19

Seven angels sound seven trumpets, bringing judgment upon the nations.

Read prayerfully the following sections.

Ch. 8:6—9:21	The judgment of God falls, as six angels sound six trumpets.
Ch. 10:1–11	The mighty angel and the little scroll.
Ch. 11:1–14	The heralds of the Second Advent are announced.
Ch. 11:15–19	The angel sounds the seventh trumpet to announce the kingdom.

Review the passage and answer these context questions.

What was man's attitude after the devastation of the earth?

What power did the witnesses have?

What will the inhabitants of the earth do to the two witnesses?

Research study questions; refer to scripture cross-references.

What might indicate that the "fallen star" is Satan? Ezek. 28:14–19; Is. 14:12; Luke 10:18. According to the book of Job, Satan appears in heaven. Job 1:6. What happens to him in Revelation?

To what might "the mystery of God" refer?

Who were the heralds of Christ's first advent? Luke 2:8–13; 3:1–6. Who are the heralds of His Second Advent? Which two men of the Old Testament fit the description?

Record your answer to these self-examination questions.

Who seals me against the woes of coming judgment?

How am I being a witness, warning all to trust in Christ for salvation?

What do others see in me that tells them the King is coming?

Respond to God in prayer and praise.

Praise God that Jesus bore our judgment. Ask for more courage to be a herald of the King. Ask for help to live now as a citizen of heaven.

Revelation 12—13

Satan's last effort to convince mankind to rebel against God.

Read prayerfully the following sections.

Ch. 12:1–17	Satan's persecution of God's people is intensified.
Ch. 13:1–10	The antichrist and his deception are described.
Ch. 13:11–18	The false prophet and his deception are described.

Review the passage and answer these context questions.

Who was the male child to whom the woman gave birth?

Against whom did the dragon finally make war?

What is called for on the part of the saints?

Research study questions; refer to scripture cross-references.

The church is never described as "travailing in birth," yet Israel is often described this way. Would this indicate to us that the "woman" described is Israel? Micah 5:2, 3.

Why does the whole world follow the beast? John 5:43; 2 Thess. 2:11.

Whom does Paul say man in his depravity would worship? Rom. 1:21–25.

Record your answer to these self-examination questions.

In what way is Christ more important to me than life itself?

How can I make sure that I am not a hindrance to God's work?

Where do I find wisdom when my foes are powerful?

Respond to God in prayer and praise.

Praise God there is still a future for Israel. Pray for greater watchfulness against all anti-christs. Pray for greater watchfulness against false prophets.

Revelation 14

John sees 144,000 delivered by the Lamb and the wicked destroyed.

Read prayerfully the following sections.

Ch. 14:1–5	John sees the Lamb with the 144,000 redeemed.
Ch. 14:6–13	John sees angels proclaim the gospel and the fall of Babylon.
Ch. 14:14–20	John sees three angels harvesting evildoers for judgment.

Review the passage and answer these context questions.

What would make the 144,000 distinct from those who are alive today?

What sort of evangelism do we read about in this chapter?

What sort of harvest takes place at this time?

Research study questions; refer to scripture cross-references.

Who is the first fruit of the resurrection? 1 Cor. 15:20. What does the term "first fruit" imply? Ex. 23:19.

What more can be learned about the mark of the beast in the following verses? Rev. 13:16–18.

Which chapter in the book of Revelation gives the clearest description of the Son of Man? When will the sixth angel reap the earth? Matt. 25:31–46.

Record your answer to these self-examination questions.

What standards does God expect from me as I follow the Lamb?

How patiently do I follow God's commandments in a sin-filled world?

In what ways can I reap souls for God's kingdom?

Respond to God in prayer and praise.

Praise God for the Lamb seen in heaven. Praise God for the angel's proclamation during tribulation. Pray that many will respond to the gospel and trust Christ.

Revelation 15—16

John sees seven angels deliver the seven last plagues.

Read prayerfully the following sections.

Ch. 15:1–4	John describes how the songs of Moses and of the Lamb are sung.
Ch. 15:5–8	John describes angels sent to bring judgment on the nations.
Ch. 16:1–21	John describes God's final judgments on the nations.

Review the passage and answer these context questions.

What do the redeemed think of God's judgments?

What did those who were judged refuse to accomplish?

Where will the last great battle be fought?

Research study questions; refer to scripture cross-references.

Why is the location of God's throne likened unto "a sea of glass"? Dan. 7:9; Zech. 9:10. How else is this throne described in a previous chapter? Rev. 4:6

Why might the temple of God, at this time, be filled with smoke so that no one could enter? Ex. 40:34, 35.

What other scriptures might indicate that these plagues and their effects might be literal? Ex. 9. What is said in Thessalonians about Jesus coming like a thief? 1 Thess. 5:1–5

Record your answer to these self-examination questions.

How is the righteousness of God revealed in me?

With what urgency am I telling people of God's judgment in these last days?

Do I really expect Jesus to come suddenly? How prepared am I?

Respond to God in prayer and praise.

Praise God that heaven sings the song of the Lamb. Pray for present-day rulers and nations. Ask for the spread of the gospel today.

Revelation 17—18

John sees the religious, political, and economic systems judged.

Read prayerfully the following sections.

Ch. 17:1–6	John's vision of an adulterous, murderous woman sitting on the beast.
Ch. 17:7–18	John's reaction and the angel's interpretation of the vision.
Ch. 18:1–5	John hears the call of God to His people to flee Babylon.
Ch. 18:6–24	John is given a description of Babylon's sins and her destruction.

Review the passage and answer these context questions.

When were the names written in the book of life?

What name is given to the great city?

What is found in the city that merited such judgment?

Research study questions; refer to scripture cross-references.

Which of the apostles mentioned Babylon in one of his epistles? 1 Pet. 5:13.

What does scripture say happened to ancient Babylon? Jer. 51:42–48. Is there a city of that name today?

What could suggest that these chapters refer to two Babylons, one religious and one commercial? Is. 21:9; Jer. 50:46.

Record your answer to these self-examination questions.

How am I bearing testimony for Jesus?

How do I show that not only am I chosen, but that I am also faithful?

How patient am I in waiting for God to judge those who have wronged His church?

Respond to God in prayer and praise.

Pray for the persecuted church. Ask for a clear understanding of God's Word. Pray for obedience to the call of God.

Revelation 19—20

Hallelujah, God reigns! The thousand years and Satan's doom are in focus.

Read prayerfully the following sections.

Ch. 19:1–10	John witnesses the praise and celebration of the marriage of the Lamb.
Ch. 19:11—20:3	John witnesses Christ's return and the battle of Armageddon.
Ch. 20:4–6	John witnesses believers being raised to reign with Christ.
Ch. 20:7–15	John witnesses Satan's destruction and the Great White Throne judgment.

Review the passage and answer these context questions.

What great sounds were heard in heaven?

What happens to the beast and the false prophet?

How many resurrections are mentioned in this chapter?

Research study questions; refer to scripture cross-references.

What group of believers is called the bride of Christ? 2 Cor. 11:2; Eph. 5:23–32.

What weapon or weapons will Christ use to defeat the armies who will be arrayed against Him? Is. 11:4.

Will believers stand before another throne of judgment? What is this judgment called? What will be judged? 2 Cor. 5:10.

Record your answer to these self-examination questions.

What can I do to be sure that I will have an invitation to this wedding?

How am I helping to make sure that none of my friends are left behind?

When did the power of the second death lose its control over me?

Respond to God in prayer and praise.

Ask for full assurance of salvation. Pray that many will be saved before these events take place. Praise God for the first resurrection.

Revelation 21—22

John hears the invitation to come as eternity is revealed.

Read prayerfully the following sections.

Ch. 21:1–27	John describes the New Jerusalem, God's holy city, built for His people.
Ch. 22:1–6	John describes the perfect life and blessings in the New Jerusalem.
Ch. 22:7–21	John is instructed not to seal the prophecy, as life is offered to all.

Review the passage and answer these context questions.

Which geographic feature will be missing on the new earth?

How long will the believer reign with Christ?

When should we expect Christ to return?

Research study questions; refer to scripture cross-references.

What does the word "new" imply? Is. 65:17; 66:22; 2 Pet. 3:10–13. Name the classes of people found in these chapters.

The angel says "we will see His face." Who does John say Christians will resemble? 1 John 3:1–3.

Who is speaking in the last division of Revelation? Comparing verse 13 of the last chapter with verse 8 of the first chapter, what conclusion can be drawn?

Record your answer to these self-examination questions.

How does God's promise of future glory enable me to live in an impure world?

How do I drink from this river of water?

Have I heeded the gospel invitation?

Respond to God in prayer and praise.

Ask for faith to look for the New Jerusalem. Praise God for eternal life. Pray for many to respond to the gospel.